HIGH
EXPECTATIONS

HIGH
EXPECTATIONS

An Action Plan
for Implementing
Goals 2000

Fred C. Lunenburg
Beverly J. Irby

CORWIN PRESS, INC.
A Sage Publications Company
Thousand Oaks, California

For information:

Corwin Press, Inc.
A Sage Publications Company
2455 Teller Road
Thousand Oaks, California 91320
E-mail: order@corwinpress.com

SAGE Publications Ltd.
6 Bonhill Street
London EC2A 4PU
United Kingdom

SAGE Publications India Pvt. Ltd.
M-32 Market
Greater Kailash I
New Delhi 110 048 India

Printed in the United States of America

Library of Congress Cataloging-in-Publication Data

Lunenburg, Frederick C.
High expectations: An action plan for implementing Goals 2000
/ by Fred C. Lunenburg, and Beverly J. Irby.
    p.   cm.
Includes bibliographical references and index.
ISBN 0-8039-6605-9 (cloth: acid-free paper)
ISBN 0-8039-6606-7 (pbk.: acid-free paper)
    1. School improvement programs—United States.   2. Educational change—United States.   3. United States. Goals 2000: Educate America Act.   I. Irby, Beverly J.   II. Title.
LB2822.82 .L85   1998
371.01'0973—ddc21   98-25464

This book is printed on acid-free paper.

99 00 01 02 03 04 05 7 6 5 4 3 2 1

Corwin Editorial Assistant: Kristen L. Gibson
Production Editor: Denise Santoyo
Editorial Assistant: Stephanie Allen
Typesetter: Lynn Miyata
Cover Designer: Michelle Lee

Contents

Preface

High Expectations offers a blueprint for helping schools and students achieve high standards. It provides school leaders with action strategies for beginning or revisiting their reform efforts. Each chapter first reviews research on areas related to each of the eight Goals 2000. Then, specific strategies for school leaders to begin or continue implementation of Goals 2000 are discussed. At the end of each chapter, references are provided to enable educators to follow up with additional reading of topics of special interest to their restructuring efforts.

Overview of Contents

Introduction. The Introduction lays the foundation and context for the book. It focuses on modern school reform, past and present, and the changes that have created organizational demands for a new approach to restructuring. We review the evolution of modern school reform over the past 50 years and set the stage for our subject: national direction through Goals 2000. These eight goals provide the framework for the book.

Chapter 1: Every Child Ready. This chapter addresses children's readiness to learn. Goal 1 implies universal access to appropriate preschool environments, parental support in the child's preschool education, and attention to health and prenatal care. The first national education goal sets the stage for a national commitment to early childhood education. We discuss four strategies for implementing Goal 1: provide developmentally appropriate preschool learning environments, include technology for special needs learners, involve parents in the education process, and provide information to parents about the importance of health and nutrition in the preparation of children for learning.

Chapter 2: Graduation Rates Increased. This chapter examines characteristics of high school dropouts, the urban schools crisis, dropout prevention, and school intervention programs. We present 10 strategies for implementing Goal 2: alter the instructional environment, enhance positive effects of school membership, develop career academies, initiate school board policies, determine students' learning styles, consider community-based organizations, establish case management intervention, create mentoring, establish a school within a school, and use negative-sanction policies.

Chapter 3: Every Student Competent. Although all the national education goals are important, increasing student achievement in the core subjects will be the ultimate test of educational reform. We discuss three strategies for implementing Goal 3: teach critical thinking, consider constructivism, and investigate current restructuring initiatives.

Chapter 4: Every Teacher Prepared. A highly talented workforce of professional educators to teach challenging subject matter is built, not born. Access to preservice teacher education and continuing professional development will provide teachers with the knowledge and skills needed to teach to an increasingly diverse student population with a variety of educational, social, and health needs. We offer six strategies for implementing Goal 4: consider Holmes Group standards, create professional development schools, develop teaching internships, consider Renaissance Group principles, reform programs for the preparation of school administrators, and emphasize professional development guidelines for upgrading professionalism among teachers and school administrators.

Chapter 5: Mathematics and Science Reform. For some time, U.S. students have not performed well in international mathematics and science comparisons. Developments are under way to reverse the consistently low performance of U.S. students in mathematics and science. The National Council of Teachers of Mathematics and the National Committee on Science Education Standards and Assessment have developed national standards that challenge traditional approaches to teaching mathematics and science. We provide three strategies for implementing Goal 5: develop a plan for integrating science and mathematics, create a plan for science and mathematics assessment, and integrate technology with mathematics and science education.

Chapter 6: Every Adult Literate. Low literacy levels exact a cost on the nation's economy and society in a variety of ways. Low levels of literacy are related to the following social problems: crime, homelessness, alcohol and drug abuse, poverty, low economic productivity of the nation, and threatened health and safety of citizens. We present two strategies for implementing Goal 6: develop an adult literacy program and establish an agenda for lifelong learning.

Chapter 7: Every School Safe. Growing violence, chaos in classrooms, and access to drugs are a regular part of the school day for an increasing number of students. Increasing the graduation rate (Goal 2), improving student achievement in challenging subject matter (Goals 3 and 5), and ensuring the ability of our students to compete in the world economy and carry out their responsibilities of citizenship (Goal 6) will be much more difficult to achieve if our schools and neighborhoods are unsafe. We discuss five strategies for implementing Goal 7: predict school violence, prevent school violence, focus resources on schools, strengthen the system, and create an orderly climate for learning.

Chapter 8: More Parents Involved. This chapter discusses seven categories of parent involvement: Gordon's systems approach, the System Development Corporation (SDC) study, Berger's role categories, Chavkin and William's parent involvement roles, Honig's early childhood education model, Jones's levels of parent involvement, Epstein's typologies, and academically supportive behaviors for Hispanic parents. Moreover, we examine six strategies for implementing Goal 8: consider developing a Center on Families program; consider the establishment of parent centers; investigate the accelerated schools movement; develop parent cooperatives; consider focusing on families, technology, and the schools; and create new options for students.

Epilogue. This brief chapter looks to the future and the challenges that will confront those who are charged with the responsibility for implementing Goals 2000. Resource A provides readers with a quick reference summary of the 39 strategies we offer in achieving *High Expectations*.

Acknowledgments

Several persons have read drafts of chapters and made helpful criticisms and suggestions: Rafael Lara-Alecio, Associate Professor of Bilingual/ESL and Multicultural Education at Texas A&M University; Scott Barrett, Director of Technology, Conroe Independent School District; Genevieve Brown, Professor and Chair, Department of Educational Leadership and Counseling, Sam Houston State University; Claudia Iselt, Principal, Spring Branch Independent School District; Charles Michel, Assistant Principal, Katy Independent School District; Clay Webb, Assistant Principal, Huntsville Independent School District; Melinda Wooderson-Perzan, Principal, Huntsville Independent School District; Dr. Alana Mraz, Director of Curriculum, Lake Forest School District; Wayne Martin Mellinger, Graduate Faculty, The Fielding Institute; and Kathryn Whittaker, Professor, University of Northern Colorado. Their input was extremely useful to us in our revisions. In addition, we wish to express special thanks to Lee Montgomery and Judith Southworth of Southern Utah University for their numerous ideas in planning this volume. Similarly, we feel a deep debt to all those other persons who conducted the studies that we have drawn on so extensively and that have guided our thinking. The references reflect the importance of their contributions.

FRED C. LUNENBURG

BEVERLY J. IRBY

About the Authors

Fred C. Lunenburg is Professor of Educational Administration in the Center for Research and Doctoral Studies in Educational Leadership at Sam Houston State University. He was previously on the faculty in educational administration at the University of Louisville. He also served as a public school teacher, principal, superintendent of schools, and university dean. He is the author of more than 75 publications on schools as organizations and on the social and psychological aspects of educational administration. His best known publications include *The Principalship: Concepts and Applications* and *Educational Administration: Concepts and Practices* (with Allan C. Ornstein). He received the Donatelli Award for Research for a series of studies on organizational climate, and he was cited in *Who's Who in Educational Administration.*

Beverly J. Irby is Associate Professor and Coordinator of Research in the Center for Research and Doctoral Studies in Educational Leadership at Sam Houston State University. She has also served as director of field experiences, supervisor of mentor services, and liaison for the Urban Professional Development Site at the university and as a Title VII grant coordinator on an urban elementary campus. Before this, she was an elementary school principal, assistant superintendent, and superintendent of schools, as well as a school psychologist, educational diagnostician, and special education director. Her research, writing, and presentations have explored the principalship, administrative portfolio development, general and women's leadership issues, personnel and program evaluation, program development in bilingual education, parent involvement, gifted education, science education, and adolescent pregnancy and parenting programs. She is the author or coauthor of numerous grants totaling $5 million and often serves as a consultant to school districts. She is a member of the International Who's Who of Women and has received the Texas Council of Women School Educators' Outstanding Educator Award and the Renaissance Group Research Fellow Award. She is coeditor or coauthor of four books on women's issues, *The Principal Portfolio* (1997), and the national training model for administrator appraisal for the National Association of Secondary School Principals.

Introduction

American society continually experiences periodic resurgences of educational reform. Over the past 50 years, there have been several significant efforts to reform schools. For example, in the 1950s the launching of Sputnik I generated national concern about our military and technological competitiveness with the Soviet Union. In response, the U.S. Congress enacted the National Defense Education Act (1958), which offered substantial financial assistance to bolster science and mathematics programs in the schools. At the same time, critics such as James Bryant Conant (1959) called for an upgrading of curricular content, instruction, and teacher preparation. He was particularly concerned that the academically talented were not being sufficiently challenged by the curriculum.

The 1960s produced serious social unrest that manifested itself in a hasty redesign of school curricula to produce "relevance" and "choices" for students. During this period, concern for the individual, minority groups, and later females raised an awareness that segments of society were not benefiting from their public school experiences. For example, the National Advisory Commission on Civil Disorders

(1967) indicted schools for perpetuating racism and inequality. Subsequently, the National Advisory Council on the Education of Disadvantaged Children (1969) earmarked schools as a major key to providing opportunities for the disadvantaged.

The 1970s saw two concurrent movements: (1) a new reform focus on the disadvantaged broadened to include multicultural, bilingual, and special education; and (2) the excesses of the liberal 1960s curricula created a "back-to-basics" movement. Instruction was focused on ensuring minimum competency and contributed to the rise of the minimum competency testing movement. The emphasis on minimum competencies fostered concern that many students were being insufficiently challenged.

The permissiveness of the 1960s and 1970s was accompanied by a downward spiral in academic standards. Nationally, test scores declined, the dropout rate increased, students selected easier courses from a broadened electives curricula, grade inflation proliferated, and textbooks were "dumbed down" by publishers. This dissatisfaction with education and reform efforts rekindled concerns over U.S. competitiveness, now economic rather than military. Policymakers felt compelled to act.

In the early 1980s, a number of commissions and task force reports warned that education in the United States was in dire need of reform. The most publicized of these efforts was the report of the National Commission on Excellence in Education titled *A Nation at Risk* (1983). It called for strengthening high school graduation requirements and admission to college, increasing standards and expectations for student performance, lengthening the school day and school year, more testing, raising teachers' salaries, and generally holding students and educators more accountable.

Until recently, it was not possible for the United States to determine whether it was making the progress needed to remain internationally competitive. America had no national goals to provide focus and consistency to determine whether education stakeholders were all working toward high-performance education results. In a number of key areas, we lacked the necessary data to judge whether we were making sufficient progress or falling further behind other industrialized nations.

The National Education Goals

In 1989, the nation's governors and the president reached agreement at an education summit convened in Charlottesville, Virginia, that, unless the nation established clear education goals and unless all education stakeholders worked cooperatively to achieve them, the United States would be unprepared to face the technological, scientific, and economic challenges of the 21st century. Recognizing that the decade of the 1990s was about to open with the information superhighway, the 1989 Education Summit led to the adoption of six national education goals that set high expectations for education performance at every stage of a learner's life, from preschool years through adulthood (Department of Education, 1991). These goals established a framework for lifelong learning—a requisite for a world of rapidly changing information.

In March 1994, Congress adopted the six goals, expanded the number to eight, and put the eight national education goals into law by enacting the Goals 2000: Educate America Act (see Box I.1).

National efforts to reform education in the past have been more fragmented than coherent. For the first time in history, school reform has a national focus, mainly due to the national goals and the high expectations they embody. In addition, for the first time in history, educators have ready access to information regarding best practices in education and critical asynchronous dialogue regarding school restructuring efforts, mainly due to recent advancements in technology, such as the Internet, distance learning, and affordable multimedia computers. Now what is needed is a strategy that empowers state and local leadership to advance reform in ways that do not refer to the national goals as symbolic icons but that deeply embed the goals in systemic, positive change.

In the following chapters, leaders will find what research says about the topic related to each goal, as well as suggestions for initiating dialogue and positive actions toward restructuring schools. It will be up to school leaders to take the suggested action plans and turn them into functional and meaningful restructuring plans for their schools and school districts.

Box I.1. The National Education Goals

Goal 1:   All children in America will start school ready to learn.

Goal 2:   The high school graduation rate will increase to at least 90%.

Goal 3:   All students will leave grades 4, 8, and 12 having demonstrated competency over challenging subject matter, including English, mathematics, science, foreign languages, civics and government, economics, arts, history, and geography; and every school in America will ensure that all students learn to use their minds well so they may be prepared for responsible citizenship, further learning, and productive employment in our nation's modern economy.

Goal 4:   The nation's teaching force will have access to programs for the continued improvement of its professional skills and the opportunity to acquire the knowledge and skills needed to instruct and prepare all American students for the next century.

Goal 5:   U.S. students will be first in the world in mathematics and science achievement.

Goal 6:   Every adult American will be literate and will possess the knowledge and skills necessary to compete in a global economy and exercise the rights and responsibilities of citizenship.

Goal 7:   Every school in the United States will be free of drugs, violence, and the unauthorized presence of firearms and alcohol and will offer a disciplined environment conducive to learning.

Goal 8:   Every school will promote partnerships that will increase parental involvement and participation in promoting the social, emotional, and academic growth of children.

References

Conant, J. B. (1959). *The American high school today.* New York: McGraw-Hill.

Department of Education. (1991). *America 2000: An education strategy.* Washington, DC: Government Printing Office.

National Advisory Commission on Civil Disorders. (1967). *Report of the National Advisory Commission on Civil Disorders.* New York: Bantam.

National Advisory Council on the Education of Disadvantaged Children. (1969). *Report of the National Advisory Council on the Education of Disadvantaged Children.* Washington, DC: Government Printing Office.

National Commission on Excellence in Education. (1983). *A nation at risk.* Washington, DC: Government Printing Office.

CHAPTER 1

Every Child Ready

By the year 2000, all children in America will start school ready to learn.
(Goals 2000: Educate America Act of 1994)

Goal 1 implies universal access to appropriate preschool environments, parental support in the child's preschool education, and attention to health and prenatal care (Lunenburg, 1992). The first national education goal and the position statement from the National Association for the Education of Young Children (NAEYC) sets the stage for a national commitment to early childhood education. NAEYC underscores developmentally appropriate preschool learning environments, the critical role parents play in the education process, and the importance of health and nutrition in the preparation of children for learning.

Research: Preschool Experiences

Preschool experiences should provide cognitive and social enrichment during early childhood development. The goal of these experiences should be to promote children's ability to make the transition to school successfully (Reynolds, 1994; Schweinhart & Weikart, 1988; Wachs & Gruen, 1982) and to prevent poor school adjustment outcomes such as school failure, unemployment, and poverty.

1

Box 1.1. What the Research Says About . . .

Preschool Experiences

- One or two years of preschool can improve children's school readiness, early scholastic achievement, and school competence, such as lower grade retention and special education placement (Barnett, 1992; Haskins, 1989; Hubbell, 1983; McKey et al., 1985; Reynolds, 1995; West, Hauskien, Chandler, & Collins, 1992; White, 1985).

- Preschool experiences reduce school dropout rate and increase employability (Berrueta-Clement, Schweinhart, Barnett, Epstein, & Weikart, 1984; Reynolds, 1994; Schweinhart, Barnes, & Weikart, 1993).

- Early attainment sets boundaries on later attainment (Alexander & Entwisle, 1988; Belsky & MacKinnon, 1994; Entwisle, Alexander, Cadigan, & Pallas, 1986).

- High-quality nonparental preschool experiences are related to positive functioning in the early elementary grades (Andersson, 1989; Belsky & MacKinnon, 1994; Field, 1991; Howes, 1988; Vandell & Corasaniti, 1990; Vandell, Henderson, & Wilson, 1988; Whitebrook, Howes, & Phillips, 1990).

Technology and Special Needs
Preschool Learners

- Technology can assist with the development of vocabulary in special needs children (Schery & O'Connor, 1992).

- Technology enables the special needs child to communicate, solve problems, write, and practice reading and listening better (Holzberg, 1994; Ward, 1990).

Applying Research to Practice: Developing an Action Plan

Educational leaders, particularly those at preschool or elementary campuses, can begin to develop specific strategies for restructuring

Family Experience and Preschool Learners

◆ Children whose parents expect them to do well in school tend to perform better than children whose parents have low expectations (Maxwell & Eller, 1994).

◆ Cognitive stimulation that children experience at home is systematically related to children's school performance (Belsky & MacKinnon, 1994; Bradley & Caldwell, 1981; Tizard, Blatchford, Burke, Farquhar, & Plewis, 1988).

◆ Parents' parenting styles (e.g., their level of warmth in interacting with their children) and marital interaction styles (i.e., negative and positive interactions) significantly predict children's kindergarten achievement (Belsky & MacKinnon, 1994; Cummings, Iannotti, & Zahn-Waxler, 1985; Emery, 1982; MacKinnon, 1989).

Health and Prenatal Care

◆ Parents' behavior (even before birth) can be an important determinant of how well their children will do in school (Mathes & Irby, 1993).

◆ Five birth characteristics linked to children's later health, behavior, and academic achievement are late (third trimester) or no prenatal care, low maternal weight gain (less than 21 pounds), mother smoked during pregnancy, mother used illicit drugs during pregnancy, and mother drank alcohol during pregnancy (Department of Health and Human Services, National Center for Health Statistics, 1996; McCormick, Gortmaker, & Sobol, 1990; National Education Goals Panel, 1994; Prince, Nord, & Zill, 1993).

◆ Low-income children are less likely to be fully immunized than others (United Nations Children's Fund, 1993).

◆ Healthy children are more likely to be ready to learn (Mathes & Irby, 1993).

their schools by reviewing the research base related to early childhood experiences and by bringing their experiential knowledge into the completion of the plan. Following are suggested action strategies related to Goal 1 that can assist educators in developing an action plan for restructuring their schools.

Strategy 1: Begin a School and District Dialogue
by Establishing Inquiry Groups to Investigate Various
Effective Early Childhood Curricular Models

School leaders should first know what is available as effective pre-school curricular programs. For dialogue to begin among faculty and community members, effective preschool experiences in the areas of curriculum and technology must be considered. Every educator knows that a valid curriculum model provides the theoretical framework needed to operate an effective early childhood education program (Lunenburg, 1995; Lunenburg & Ornstein, 1996) and to provide opportunities for children to be ready to learn.

We suggest that educational leaders consider six widely known early childhood curriculum models: Bank Street's developmental-interaction approach, Teaching Strategies' Creative Curriculum, the High/Scope Curriculum, the Kamii-DeVries constructivist approach, the Montessori method, and the direct instruction model. In addition, we suggest two technology-related models for integrating into the early childhood curriculum: Different and Same and Writing to Read and VALE. We recognize that these are not all-inclusive; however, this listing is provided to assist leaders in beginning to shape a dialogue around effective early childhood curricular models. Brief summaries of the distinctive features of each model follow (Epstein, Schweinhart, & McAdoo, 1997).

The Bank Street
Developmental-Interaction Approach

This approach is named for the Bank Street College of Education in New York City, which offers graduate degrees in education. Influenced by the educational philosophy of John Dewey, Lucy Sprague Mitchell formulated the approach's central tenet of development of the whole child through active learning. From 1928 on, Barbara Biber used psychodynamic theory to shape the approach. Later, Bank Street formulated a curriculum model for the federal Follow Through early education project. Bank Street encourages teachers to use their own judgment about educational practices in light of their understanding and observation of children's development (Biber, 1984; Zimiles, 1993).

The Creative Curriculum
of Teaching Strategies

The Creative Curriculum was developed by Diana Trister Dodge, based on her career in working with early childhood educators. The approach helps teachers make their practices consistent with their goals for children by arranging their classrooms to support teachers' developmentally appropriate practice and children's active learning, which is directed toward their social competence. Teachers arrange the learning environment into 10 interest areas: art, blocks, cooking, computers, house corner, library corner, music and movement, the outdoors, sand and water, and table toys. Dodge first presented the Creative Curriculum in 1979, then expanded it in 1988 and again in 1992, founding Teaching Strategies, Inc., for this purpose. Creative Curriculum specialists acknowledge that support by trainers is desirable; however, teachers learn the Creative Curriculum primarily through self-instruction rather than through training (Dodge, 1988; Dodge & Colker, 1992).

The High/Scope Curriculum

The High/Scope Curriculum was developed in the 1960s and 1970s by the High/Scope Educational Research Foundation staff, led by David P. Weikart (Hohmann, Banet, & Weikart, 1979; Hohmann & Weikart, 1995). Based on Piaget's constructivist theory of child development, the High/Scope Curriculum initially focused on disadvantaged preschool children. The approach now encompasses all children and every type of early childhood setting. The High/Scope Curriculum advocates active learning and classrooms arranged with discrete, well-equipped interest areas. Each day, children engage in a consistent routine that consists of time for children to plan, carry out, and reflect on their own learning as well as time to engage in small- and large-group activities. Adults support children's active learning by organizing the environment and establishing a consistent daily routine; establishing a supportive social climate; encouraging children's intentional activities, problem solving, and verbal reflections; planning small- and large-group learning experiences; and interpreting children's actions in terms of the High/Scope key experiences in child development. High/Scope has identified 58 key experiences in child development for the preschool years. The key experiences are grouped into 10 categories: creative representation, language and literacy, initiative and social relations, movement, music, classification, seriation, number, and space and time.

The Kamii-DeVries Constructivist Perspective

The Kamii-DeVries constructivist perspective was developed by Constance Kamii and Rheta DeVries (DeVries & Kohlberg, 1990; Kamii & DeVries, 1980, 1993). The perspective is based on the Piagetian constructivist principle that children develop their knowledge, intelligence, morality, and personality from their interactions with the world within a logical-mathematical framework. Physical activity provides a vehicle through which children learn through mental action. A child-centered approach is used by teachers who are well grounded in traditional early childhood education. Teachers prepare the setting for active learning, remain in touch with what children are thinking, respond to children on their perspective, and help children extend their ideas.

The Montessori Method

The Montessori Method was developed by Maria Montessori (Lindauer, 1993; Montessori, 1964), a physician working with poor children in Italy. The Montessori method—which aims at developing children's senses, academic skills, practical life skills, and character—is the world's oldest extant early childhood curriculum model and is used today by Montessori teachers throughout the world. Montessori teachers carefully prepare program settings, filling them with Montessori materials, which are designed to encourage children to learn on their own. There is a precise way for children to use each set of materials to learn a particular concept or skill. Montessori teachers show children how to use the materials, then let the children select which ones they will use, expecting them to return the materials to assigned places when they are finished.

The Direct Instruction Model

The model began with the preschool program devoted to behavioral learning principles operated by Carl Bereiter and Siegfried

Englemann (1966) at the University of Illinois at Urbana in the mid-1960s. The model was expanded to Follow Through early education programs and resulted in the Distar materials published by Science Research Associates. Direct instruction focuses on academics, specifically the content of intelligence and achievement tests. In direct instruction, teachers lead small groups of children in precisely planned 20-minute question-and-answer lessons in language, mathematics, and reading. The classroom is kept free of distracting materials. The developers have discovered that direct instruction suits elementary school teachers better than it suits preschool teachers. The model seeks to perfect the teacher's teacher-centered approach rather than to convert the educator to learner-centered education.

Different and Same:
A Video-Based Curriculum

Different and Same is a supplementary curriculum developed by the company that produces *Mr. Rogers' Neighborhood*. This curriculum, including nine videos and accompanying instructional material, is directed at helping children in the early years and grades identify and prevent prejudice. Teachers who have used this curriculum have found that the videos provide a rich stimulus for enlightening children about the value of diversity, as well as the realities of prejudice and racism within their world.

The central characters are animal puppets that are exposed to situations involving exclusion, name calling, and stereotyping. The adult characters are played by humans from various ethnic and racial backgrounds. The enrichment activities are centered around diversity in problem solving and cooperative learning. This technology-based curriculum is also recommended for special education classes (Lucero, 1997).

Writing to Read and VALE

Writing to Read 2000 (English version) and VALE (Spanish version for limited-English-proficient students), effective developmental early childhood curricula validated by the Educational Testing Service (ETS), were developed for IBM by John Henry Martin, teacher, principal, superintendent, and professor (IBM Solutions, 1997). These programs integrate listening, speaking, reading, and writing while capitalizing on children's natural desire to communicate. The curricula centers around thematic units, computer centers, work journal centers, writing/typing centers, make words centers, tape library centers, and activity centers. Writing to Read 2000 and VALE promote parent participation through reading and writing with their children (http://www.solutions.ibm.com/k12/).

Strategy 2: Include Technological Considerations for Special Needs Learners

Leaders need to consider the special needs, including technological needs, of all learners in plans for restructuring. There are now numerous technology-based learning activities for children in their early years of which leaders and early childhood programs can take advantage.

Technology can assist with the development of language and speech in special needs children as early as 1 year old (Thode, 1998). It enables special needs children to communicate, solve problems, write, and practice reading and listening better. Technology is a motivational tool for these children (Thode, 1998). As illustrated in Box 1.2, using a simple technology switch connected to a light box afforded one young child the opportunity to demonstrate that she knew that when she pressed the switch she could communicate.

It is necessary to bring technology into the lives of special needs learners earlier and to inform and provide parents with such devices to equip them to be able to communicate with their children. If these devices are remarkably productive for the physically and mentally challenged children, they can also be so for nonchallenged children. Early childhood administrators need to facilitate the use of these technological advances in the early years for children and their parents to promote a readiness to learn.

Strategy 3: Involve the Parents to Promote Readiness to Learn

Leaders can offer some specific suggestions for parents to consider in the early childhood years to promote readiness to learn. A few suggestions follow (Education Excellence Partnership, 1994; Lara-Alecio, Irby, & Ebener, 1997):

1. *Read to preschool children at least 20 minutes a day.* Regular reading to children is one of the most important activities parents can

Box 1.2. A Vignette:
An Early Childhood Experience—Ready to Learn

When adaptive technology for the physically and mentally challenged was just emerging in the mid to late 1980s, one of the authors had the opportunity to observe a speech therapist working with a multichallenged child. In this session, a simple cheek switch was attached to the wheelchair, and the switch was connected to a four-quadrant light box. The speech therapist had prepared an overlay for the light box, which had in one quadrant a smiley face, in another quadrant a frowning face, in a third quadrant, a picture of the child with a sentence that read, "Hi, my name is Toya," and in the fourth quadrant a blank space. Toya was at the time approximately 12 years old and had never spoken a word. This author was privileged to hear this child utter her first communication with adaptive technology through a simple switch and a light box. The therapist asked, "Can you tell me your name?" Slowly and tediously, the child's cheek touched the switch; her palsied jerks attempted to move her gaze from the box, but sheer determination kept her focused. The light bumped from one quadrant to another, until it rested on, "Hello, my name is Toya." A big grin beamed on the child's face, and the therapist asked, "How does Toya feel right now?" Again in deliberate head movements, Toya slowly moved the light from quadrant to quadrant with the switch. The light stopped and shone through the smiley face. Toya was saying, "I am very happy." This is but one example of how simple adaptive technology helped a special needs child at age 12 to communicate her thoughts and words for the first time. What else could she have been saying had this technology been available at an earlier age?

do with their children to improve their readiness for school, serve as their child's first teacher, and instill a love of books and reading.

2. *Keep good books, magazines, and newspapers in the house; the home can mirror the school in this respect.* Make it easy—for both adults and children—to find something interesting to read.

3. *Add to children's enjoyment of reading by discussing each book they read.* Discussing the book familiarizes children with story components such as character, plot, action, and sequence and helps them associate language with printed text. Offer them computer-assisted games that promote language, writing, mathematics, and thinking.

4. *Make sure children see parents or the caregiver read for at least 20 minutes a day.* Remember, parents are a child's first teacher.

5. *If a parent has difficulty reading, tell children stories.* Telling stories is another important way that parents can participate in shared literacy activities with their children. In some cultures, storytelling and oral traditions play a more central role than reading books aloud.

6. *Limit children's television viewing to no more than 2 hours a day.* Studies indicate that although some television viewing every day is all right, excessive time watching television is directly linked to poor school performance. Watch the program with the child, then discuss the program and its implications in simple lessons.

7. *Know what kind of homework is expected from teachers, and make sure children complete it.* The more involved you are in your children's schoolwork, the more involved your children will be. Provide children with a regular, quiet place where they can do homework. Set up a place with few distractions, but close enough so they can ask you questions. Technology, through local and national service companies, now affords individual campuses the luxury of having homework hotlines, school announcements, and individualized teacher messages for parents to call.

8. *Demonstrate commitment to high standards.* Don't ask teachers to give children grades or promotions they have not earned. The goal is a good education, not a good report card. Have high expectations of children. Encourage them and tell them that "You can do it!" Words can be strengthening or demoralizing.

9. *Support school efforts to develop and maintain rules for student discipline.* Children thrive in an environment where they know what is expected of them.

10. *Help interest children in learning outside of the school day.* Find out about after-school and summer programs in the community. School leaders need to avail parents of such programs or assist them in beginning a few for the children on their campuses.

Strategy 4: Provide Information to Parents on Health and Prenatal Experiences

Leaders in schools must move beyond the four walls of the school in their reform efforts. They need to work with local and state governmental agencies to ensure that young parents receive information on prenatal and proper baby care because those factors influence later learning. Healthy children are more likely to be ready to learn.

Leaders can involve community and government entities as partners. Such entities include state health and human services, March of Dimes, community day care, Head Start, the YMCA. Others can be brainstormed as appropriate to a particular community.

One curricular model that could be considered for young parent training is found in *The Teen Pregnancy and Parenting Handbook* (Mathes & Irby, 1993b) and the accompanying *Discussion Guide* (Mathes & Irby, 1993a). These books were designed primarily as a curriculum for pregnant and parenting teens. To make an informed decision about pregnancy and parenting, pregnant teenagers need up-to-date facts on what pregnancy and parenting involve. They need to know how to take care of themselves while they are pregnant, what labor and delivery involve, and how to care for their babies after giving birth. Included in this is the need to understand the huge effect their decision to parent will have on their babies' lives. They need to be aware that quality care includes not only providing for a child's basics but also setting up the environment to ensure verbal and physical stimulation and responding to the child's cues. This curriculum was written in an effort to convey this information. Additional curriculum supplements can be found at the National Coalition for the Prevention of Adolescent Pregnancy's Web site, www.cfoc.org/ncptg.html, or by writing the National Organization for Pregnancy, Prevention, and Parenting at 4421-A East West Highway, Bethesda, MD 20814. Additional programs that can be used are *The Practical Parenting Series* and *Systematic Training for Effective Parenting (The STEP)*.

The national goal stating that all children in America will start school ready to learn is the critical foundation of Goals 2000. Only when leaders of early childhood programs adopt valid curriculum models and facilitate work with parents and community entities will we be able to examine and fulfill the educational potential of the preschool experiences of our children and early childhood programs.

References

Alexander, K. L., & Entwisle, D. R. (1988). Achievement in the first 2 years of school: Patterns and processes. *Monographs of the Society for Research in Child Development, 53*, 1-157.

Andersson, B. E. (1989). The importance of public day care for preschool children's later development. *Child Development, 60*, 857-866.

Barnett, W. S. (1992). Benefits of compensatory preschool education. *Journal of Human Resources, 27*, 279-312.

Belsky, J., & MacKinnon, C. (1994). Transition to school: Developmental trajectories and school experiences. *Early Education and Development, 5*, 106-119.

Bereiter, C., & Engelmann, S. (1966). *Teaching disadvantaged children in the preschool.* Englewood Cliffs, NJ: Prentice Hall.

Berrueta-Clement, J. R., Schweinhart, L. J., Barnett, W. S., Epstein, A. S., & Weikart, D. P. (1984). *Changed lives: The affects of the Perry Preschool Program on youths through age 19.* Ypsilanti, MI: High/Scope.

Biber, B. (1984). *Early education and psychological development.* New Haven, CT: Yale University Press.

Bradley, R., & Caldwell, B. M. (1981). The home inventory: A validation of the preschool scale for black children. *Child Development, 52*, 708-710.

Cummings, E., Iannotti, R., & Zahn-Waxler, C. (1985). Influence of conflict between adults on the emotions and aggression of young children. *Developmental Psychology, 21*, 495-507.

Department of Health and Human Services, National Center for Health Statistics. (1996). *Health, United States, 1995: Prevention objectives* (DHHS Publication No. PHS 96-1236). Washington, DC: Government Printing Office.

DeVries, R., & Kohlberg, L. (1990). *Constructivist early education: Overview and comparison with other programs.* Washington, DC: National Association for the Education of Young Children.

Dodge, D. T. (1988). *A guide for supervisors and trainers on implementing the Creative Curriculum for early childhood* (2nd ed.). Washington, DC: Teaching Strategies.

Dodge, D. T., & Colker, L. J. (1992). *The Creative Curriculum for early childhood* (3rd ed.). Washington, DC: Teaching Strategies.

Education Excellence Partnership. (1994). *Moving America to the head of the class: 50 simple things to do.* Washington, DC: Author.

Emery, E. (1982). Interparental conflict and the children of discord and divorce. *Psychological Bulletin, 92,* 310-330.

Entwisle, D., Alexander, K., Cadigan, D., & Pallas, A. (1986). The schooling process in first grade: Two samples a decade apart. *American Educational Research Journal, 23,* 587-613.

Epstein, A. S., Schweinhart, L. J., & McAdoo, L. (1997). *Models of early childhood education.* Ypsilanti, MI: High/Scope.

Field, T. (1991). Quality infant day care and grade school behavior and performance. *Child Development, 62,* 863-870.

Haskins, R. (1989). Beyond metaphor: The efficacy of early childhood education. *American Psychologist, 44,* 274-282.

Hohmann, M., Banet, B., & Weikart, D. P. (1979). *Young children in action: A manual for preschool educators.* Ypsilanti, MI: High/Scope.

Hohmann, M., & Weikart, D. P. (1995). *Educating young children: Active learning practices for preschool and child care programs.* Ypsilanti, MI: High/Scope.

Holzberg, C. S. (1994). Teacher tested ideas: Hypermedia projects that really work. *Technology and Learning, 14,* 31-34,36.

Howes, C. (1988). Relations between early child care and schooling. *Developmental Psychology, 24,* 53-57.

Hubbell, R. (1983). *A review of Head Start since 1970.* Washington, DC: Department of Health and Human Services.

IBM Solutions. (1997). *Writing to Read and VALE* [On-line]. Available: http://www.solutions.ibm.com/k12/

Kamii, C., & DeVries, R. (1980). *Group games in early education: Implications of Piaget's theory.* Washington, DC: National Association for the Education of Young Children.

Kamii, C., & DeVries, R. (1993). *Physical knowledge in preschool education: Implications of Piaget's theory.* New York: Teachers College Press.

Lara-Alecio, R., Irby, B. J., & Ebener, R. (1997). Developing academically supportive behaviors among Hispanic parents: What elementary school teachers and supervisors can do. *Preventing School Failure, 42*(1), 27-32.

Lindauer, S. L. K. (1993). Montessori education for young children. In J. L. Roopnarine & J. E. Johnson (Eds.), *Approaches to early childhood education* (2nd ed., pp. 243-259). New York: Macmillan.

Lucero, E. (1997). Promoting multiculturalism in the early grades. *Principal, 76*(5), 5-11.

Lunenburg, F. C. (1992). The urban superintendent's role in school reform. *Education and Urban Society, 25*(1), 30-44.

Lunenburg, F. C. (1995). *The principalship: Concepts and applications.* Englewood Cliffs, NJ: Prentice Hall.

Lunenburg, F. C., & Ornstein, A. O. (1996). *Educational administration: Concepts and practices.* Belmont, CA: Wadsworth.

MacKinnon, C. E. (1989). An observational investigation of sibling interactions in married and divorced families. *Developmental Psychology, 25,* 36-44.

Mathes, P. G., & Irby, B. J. (1993a). *Discussion guide. The teen pregnancy and parenting handbook.* Champaign, IL: Research Press.

Mathes, P. G., & Irby, B. J. (1993b). *The teen pregnancy and parenting handbook.* Champaign, IL: Research Press.

Maxwell, K. L., & Eller, S. K. (1994, September). Children's transition to kindergarten. *Young Children,* pp. 56-63.

McCormick, M., Gortmaker, S. L., & Sobol, A. M. (1990). Very low birthweight children: Behavior problems and school failure in a national sample. *Journal of Pediatrics, 117*(5), 687-693.

McKey, R. H., Condelli, L., Ganson, H., Barrett, B. J., McConkey, C., & Plantz, M. C. (1985). *The impact of Head Start on children, families, and communities* (DHHS Publication No. OHDS 85-31193). Washington, DC: Government Printing Office.

Montessori, M. (1964). *The Montessori method.* New York: Schocken.

National Education Goals Panel. (1994). *The National Education Goals report: Building a nation of learners.* Washington, DC: Government Printing Office.

Prince, C., Nord, C. W., & Zill, N. (1993, April). *Social indicators predictive of school success: Linking health and social information available at birth to measures of children's health, behavior, and academic status.* Paper presented at the annual meeting of the American Educational Research Association, Atlanta, GA.

Practical parenting series [Videotape]. (Available from Research Press, Dept. 97, P.O. Box 9177, Champaign, IL 61826)

Reynolds, A. J. (1994). Effects of a preschool plus follow-up intervention for children. *Developmental Psychology, 30*(6), 787-804.

Reynolds, A. J. (1995). One year of preschool intervention or two: Does it matter? *Early Childhood Research Quarterly, 10,* 1-31.

Schery, T. K., & O'Connor, L. C. (1992). The effectiveness of school-based computer language intervention with severely handicapped children. *Language, Speech, and Hearing Services in Schools, 23*(1), 43-47.

Schweinhart, L. J., Barnes, H. V., & Weikart, D. P. (1993). *Significant benefits: The High/Scope Perry preschool study through age 27.* Ypsilanti, MI: High/Scope.

Schweinhart, L. J., & Weikart, D. P. (1988). The High/Scope Perry preschool program. In R. H. Price, E. L. Cowen, R. P. Lorion, & J. Ramos-McKay (Eds.), *14 ounces of prevention: A casebook for practitioners* (pp. 53-65). Washington, DC: American Psychological Association.

Systematic training for effective parenting. [Videotapes]. (Available from American Guidance Service, Circle Pines, MN, 55041)

Thode, B. (1998). *Technology: Teacher's resource guide* (2nd ed.). Cincinnati, OH: South-West.

Tizard, B., Blatchford, P., Burke, J., Farquhar, C., & Plewis, I. (1988). *Young children at school in the inner city.* Hillsdale, NJ: Lawrence Erlbaum.

United Nations Children's Fund (UNICEF). (1993). *The progress of nations.* New York: Author.

Vandell, D., & Corasaniti, J. (1990). Child care and the family: Complex contributions to child development. *New Directions in Child Development, The Social Ecology of Day Care, 49,* 7-22.

Vandell, D., Henderson, V., & Wilson, K. (1988). A longitudinal study of children with day-care experiences of varying quality. *Child Development, 59,* 1286-1292.

Wachs, T. D., & Gruen, G. E. (1982). *Early experience and human development.* New York: Plenum.

Ward, C.D. (1990). Possibilities at their fingertips. *Dimensions, 18*(4), 7-9.

West, J., Hauskien, E., Chandler, K., & Collins, M. (1992). *Experiences in child care and early childhood programs of first and second graders prior to entering first grade. Statistics in brief.* Washington, DC: Department of Education, Office of Educational Research and Improvement.

White, K. R. (1985). Efficacy of early intervention. *Journal of Special Education, 19,* 401-416.

Whitebrook, M., Howes, C., & Phillips, D. (1990). *Who cares? Child care teachers and the quality of care in America.* Final Report of

the National Child Care Staffing Study. Oakland, CA: Child Care
    Employee Project.
Zimiles, H. (1993). The Bank Street approach. In J. L. Roopnarine &
    J. E. Johnson (Eds.), *Approaches to early childhood education*
    (2nd ed., pp. 261-273). New York: Macmillan.

CHAPTER 2

Graduation Rates Increased

*By the year 2000, the high school graduation rate
will increase to at least 90%.*
(Goals 2000: Educate America Act of 1994)

Dropping out of high school is a serious national problem that has social and economic implications for individuals and for society. For example, dropouts currently cost the United States an estimated $250 billion annually in lost earnings, taxes, and social services. Dropouts constitute 52% of those who receive welfare or are unemployed, 82% of the prison population, and 85% of the juveniles in court (Hodgkinson, 1996). Furthermore, dropouts have lower rates of intergenerational mobility (Levin, 1972; McNeal, 1995), lower levels of academic skills (Alexander, Natriello, & Pallas, 1985; McDill, Natriello, & Pallas, 1985; McNeal, 1995; Natriello, McDill, & Pallas, 1990), and poorer levels of mental health (Levin, 1972; McNeal, 1995; Rumberger, 1987) and physical health (McNeal, 1995; Rumberger, 1987) than do nondropouts.

In the past 35 years the dropout rate has improved, but it still remains at a crisis level. The average high school attrition rate in 1960 was 32%. It decreased to 21% in 1970, but by 1980 it had increased to 26%. Since 1980, the national average has fluctuated yearly; in 1995, approximately one fourth of all high school students dropped out of school before graduation (National Center for Education Statistics, 1996). American leaders must begin to address the dropout problem on a broad and substantial scale if we are to reach the goal of a 90% high school graduation rate by the year 2000.

Box 2.1. What the Research Says About . . .

Dropouts and Retention

◆ Grade retention is the single most sensitive indicator of dropout potential in high school (Kreitzer, Madaus, & Haney, 1989).

◆ One year's retention can increase the dropout risk by 45% to 50%; retaining students in two grades increases the risk as much as 90% (Mann, 1986).

Parents and Dropouts

◆ Pregnancy is often cited as the reason for leaving school among female dropouts (Mott & Marsigolio, 1985).

◆ The majority of dropouts' parents never completed high school and are either unemployed or employed in lower-status jobs (Altman, 1995).

◆ The median annual income differential for families of high school dropouts compared to the median income of families of high school graduates is about $22,000 (National Center for Education Statistics, 1996).

SES, Ethnicity, Urban Schools, and Dropouts

◆ Thirty percent of all poor children are enrolled in the 50 largest urban school districts in the nation.

◆ Teacher shortages in urban schools are 2 1/2 times greater than the national average.

◆ One third of all urban school buildings are more than 50 years old.

◆ Urban children are half as likely as their suburban counterparts to have access to preschool programs.

◆ Seventy percent of the enrollment in the typical urban district is African American, Hispanic, and Asian, but 70% of the teachers are white; 12.5% of urban school children are limited-English proficient (Clayton, 1991; Council of the Great City Schools, 1992).

Research: Characteristics of High School Dropouts

Many studies have been conducted to determine who drops out and why. Although numerous reasons have been given, poor academic

- ◆ The median urban school system Scholastic Aptitude Test (SAT) composite score is 862, compared to a national average of 904; and the urban school dropout rate is nearly 70% higher than in either suburban or rural schools (Council of the Great City Schools, 1992).

- ◆ Nearly one in three American schoolchildren will fall within the Census Bureau's designation of minority by the year 2000 (Bureau of the Census, 1991a, 1991b).

- ◆ According to the Population Reference Bureau (1995), the number of school-age immigrant children in America has risen to between 2.4 and 2.9 million, with the largest numbers of immigrants coming from Mexico, Asia, Central and South America, and the Caribbean.

- ◆ The problem of retaining and attracting middle classes of whatever racial and ethic group back to the inner cities will become difficult if not impossible to achieve (Hodgkinson, 1996).

- ◆ By 2010, 32.6 million of the nation's 62.6 million children will be in only nine states: Texas, California, Florida, New York, Illinois, Georgia, Michigan, Ohio, and Pennsylvania. Some of these nine states will have little ethnic diversity; California, Texas, and Florida will gain 1.8 million youth. More than one half of the youth population in these three states will be non-white before 2010 (Hodgkinson, 1992).

- ◆ The makeup of teachers in California, Texas, and Florida is not representative of the racial and ethnic diversity of the school-age youth. Whereas over one half of all students in these three states will be nonwhite in 2010, about 19% of the teachers in California, 15% in Florida, and 22% in Texas will be nonwhite (Hodgkinson, 1996).

- ◆ These three states have among the highest dropout rates in the nation (Hodgkinson, 1992).

performance, absenteeism, discipline problems, and grade retention have been consistently associated with high school attrition (Baldwin, Moffett, & Lane, 1992; Manning & Baruth, 1995; Praport, 1993; Ruff, 1993). For many of these potential dropouts, poor academic performance begins early in their school experiences. Often they come to school lacking basic skills prerequisite to learning. For others, success in school is neither an individual, a family, nor a cultural priority.

Applying Research to Practice: Developing an Action Plan

As school leaders consider plans for dropout prevention, they may begin with an overall plan such as the Carnegie renewal plan, which is organized around four key priorities: (1) affirm that all students can learn, even those from the most disadvantaged backgrounds; (2) build an effective governance structure with school-based management designed to eliminate many bureaucratic regulations now in existence; (3) introduce at every school a set of procedures that will help students achieve success, such as early intervention, creating smaller schools to overcome the sense of anonymity some students feel, flexible scheduling to allow weekend and work-study programs, an extended school year, new or refurbished buildings and updated learning materials, and 5- or 6-year diploma options; and (4) create a network of support beyond the school involving parents, university professors, business leaders, and government officials (Carnegie Foundation for the Advancement of Teaching, 1988).

The importance of dropout prevention as a high-priority item on the national agenda has resulted in several plans and programs to address the issue. We identify 10 additional strategies that assist in dropout prevention, related to the instructional environment, school membership, career academies, school board policies, learning styles, community-based collaboratives, case management intervention, mentoring networks, school within a school, and negative sanction policies.

Strategy 1: Alter the Instructional Environment

A primary strategy for dropout prevention is to begin to assess current practices in classrooms. Teachers need to be aware of at-risk student research findings and best practices employed with the students. Following is an overview of information so that teachers can begin to assess their own classroom practices and alter their instructional environments.

At-risk students perceive that they are treated differently from high-achieving students. Thomas Good (1987) and others (Lehr & Harris, 1991) reviewed the literature on the differential treatment of high-achieving and low-achieving students by their teachers. This differential treatment is harmful to at-risk students. Frequently these students

- Are called on less often
- Are given less wait time to answer questions
- Are rewarded for inappropriate behavior or incorrect answers
- Are questioned primarily at the knowledge or comprehension levels
- Are criticized more often for failure
- Are given less praise
- Are given less feedback
- Are interrupted more often
- Are given fewer opportunities to learn new material
- Demand less
- Evidence less acceptance and use of ideas
- Are given less eye contact and other nonverbal communication of responsiveness

The aforementioned teacher behaviors define a pattern of diminished expectations for at-risk students' ability to learn. At-risk students sense the teacher's lower regard for their personal worth as learners, come to believe it, and live up to those expectations (Acheson & Gall, 1998; Bucci & Reitzammer, 1992).

Strategy 2: Establish Effective School Membership

In a study of schools with lower than expected dropout rates, Wehlage, Rutter, Smith, Lesko, and Fernandez (1989) determined that successful schools try to create a sense of membership for at-risk students. Membership, according to Wehlage et al., depends on social bonding—the extent to which an individual forms meaningful and satisfying links with significant others in the school environment.

Students interact with their school environment by developing relationships with teachers, peers, and the school itself. Principals can strengthen student social bonding to school by strengthening positive interactions within these three relationships.

Strengthen Students' Connections to Teachers

When students believe teachers care about them, they are more inclined to want to conform to the standards for achievement and behavior established by the school. To promote this bonding, teachers can (1) establish mentoring relationships, (2) create small communities of support, and (3) make a commitment to all students regardless of background.

Strengthen Students' Connections to Peers

A second strategy for strengthening student bonding to school involves students' relationships with peers. The following can create strong peer bonds: (1) encourage participation in cocurricular activities, (2) socialize new students into the culture of the school, and (3) engage students in peer mentoring programs.

Strengthen Students' Connections to the School

A third strategy for strengthening student's bonding to school is linking the student to the school itself. Techniques that link students to school include (1) make school rules explicit, fair, and equitable and apply them consistently; (2) establish social contracts as a means of discipline; (3) give students some control over their environment; and (4) socialize students into the school early (Arhar, 1992; Lincoln & Higgins, 1991).

Strategy 3: Develop Career Academies

Career academies, for the most part, have emerged in urban school districts, where the dropout rate and unemployment are high. As a result, their primary goal has been to serve students at risk of leaving high school before graduation (Archer, Weinbaum, & Montesano, 1989; Burnett, 1992; Stern, Raby, & Dayton, 1992). Many students recruited for academies have come from poor backgrounds, have poor attendance records and grades, and have not accumulated sufficient course credit in their studies to progress in their grade level. Academies are nearly evenly divided between males and females and contain high percentages of African American and Hispanic students (Burnett, 1992; Dayton, Weisberg, & Stern, 1989).

Most career academies across the country share a number of attributes. In general, they (1) are organized as schools within schools, with a small community of students and a small, self-contained set of 5 to 10 counselors and teachers—one of whom acts as the program's "lead teacher"; (2) recruit students to volunteer for the program; (3) focus on broadly defined career themes, such as computers, electronics, or health, rather than on the job-specific outlines of traditional vocational education; (4) choose career areas with growing demands and with good employment opportunities in the local market; (5) integrate academic and vocational curricula and use block scheduling to keep students together in cohort groups throughout the day and throughout the entire 3- or 4-year program; (6) eliminate tracking by setting rigorous academic courses into the context of occupational training, giving students the option to continue their education after graduation; (7) make work experience a component of the educational process by systematically exposing students to job interviews and issues of work ethics and behavior; (8) are sustained by high levels of involvement by local businesses, as well as strong parental support; and (9) receive significant outside funding from both business and government sources (Burnett, 1992; Dayton et al., 1989; Stern et al., 1992).

Because academy students progress as a group, classes from the beginning to the end of the entire 3- or 4-year program can be designed as a sequence rather than as an assortment of unrelated units (Burnett, 1992; Stern et al., 1992). Such programwide coordination, enhanced by the academy's small class size and cohesive student body, allows the creation of strong career development programs. Career academies typically integrate academic and vocational courses— preparing students for college as well as for careers. All classes— technical as well as academic—combine the cognitive rigor of academics with the hands-on orientation of vocational training. Academies generate consistently higher expectations for student success, and students in the academies must meet all state and local requirements for graduation (Archer et al., 1989; Burnett, 1992).

Strategy 4: Develop Appropriate and Supportive School Board Policies

To help at-risk students graduate from high school, school boards can establish appropriate and supportive policies. Below are some specific suggestions to keep at-risk students in school (VanderMolen & Nolan, 1993):

1. *Require central office administrators to make programs for at-risk students an ongoing priority.* School district goals should include measurable objectives for helping at-risk students. The objectives might include raising the graduation rate, improving participation in cocurricular activities, and lowering absenteeism.

2. *Require district-level administrators to assign the same quality of staff for at-risk programs as for other school programs.* In many school districts, at-risk programs become dumping grounds for faculty members and students.

3. *Hold administrators, faculty, and students accountable for the quality of at-risk programs.* Frequently, school boards do not demand the same level of quality for alternative schools as for regular high schools. Make sure that alternative high schools have the same access to technological equipment as do regular high schools.

4. *Insist that all school district departments provide equal services to at-risk students.* At-risk students should have the same access to support services—transportation, graduation activities, and so on—as the general student population.

5. *Permit alternative methods for meeting curriculum requirements.* For example, if the school district requires students to demonstrate 85% proficiency on mathematics competency tests, teachers of at-risk students should develop individual education programs for students to reach the same goal. New asynchronous learning interactions through the Internet allow for open learning; that is, the student decides when, where, and how to interact with the learning community (Bazeli & Heintz, 1997).

6. *Permit budget flexibility for alternative programs.* Most school districts base budget allocations for a fiscal year on enrollments as of a specific date—generally at the beginning of the school year. Enrollment in the at-risk program increases throughout the year, however, as students who cannot meet the standards in the regular school transfer into the alternative school program.

7. *Permit flexibility in scheduling.* Most states require a minimum number of minutes of classroom instruction to fulfill graduation requirements. Without deviating from the state's requirements, permit at-risk students flexibility in meeting them.

Strategy 5: Determine the Students' Learning Style

Knowledge of a student's learning type can help teachers in retaining at-risk students. One instrument that can assist in determining this is the Myers-Briggs type indicator (MBTI; Myers-Briggs, 1962, 1975), based on Carl Jung's (1923) theory of psychological type. The MBTI identifies the predominant manner of intaking, processing, and outputting information. It yields 16 different type combinations from four basic preferences: extroversion or introversion (EI), sensing or intuition (SN), thinking or feeling (TF), and judgment or perception (JP). Separate studies show that student interest, application, and academic success are positively related to the presentation of material that is congruent with the individual's learning style (Carbo, 1984, 1987a, 1987b; Hengstler, Reichard, Uhl, & Goldman, 1981; Kiersey & Bates, 1978; Maxwell, 1981; McCaulley & Natter, 1974; Robyak & Patton, 1977; Nisbet, Ruble, & Schurr, 1981; Van, 1992).

Conventional school settings typically address the learning style of the introverted-intuitive-thinking-judging student. The opposite of this type, the extroverted-sensing-feeling-perception pupil, is at risk of dropping out (Kiersey & Bates, 1978; Van, 1992). The extrovert's need for the company of others often takes priority over individual study. The sensor values application over theory. Feeling students crave personal involvement, which is incongruent with didactic forms of instruction. Perception learners have difficulty reaching closure and do not function well in formally structured classrooms. Perception individuals require assistance in developing listening, critical thinking, and decision-making skills and in accepting academic routine and classroom structure (Nisbet et al., 1982; Van, 1992).

In review of the aforementioned research on learning style compatibility with conventional academic milieus, what can teachers do to accommodate the high-risk student? Classroom instruction that addresses the various learning styles of students increases the chances of scholastic success for all learners (Lawrence, 1979; McCaulley, 1981; Nisbet et al., 1982; Van, 1992). Modifications in the curriculum and teaching methods can be made so that the full spectrum of learning styles can be accommodated (Van, 1992). Of course, other learning style instruments and research, such as Gardner (1985) and Dunn and Dunn (1992a, 1992b), could be investigated by school leaders to determine learning type or style of the students.

Strategy 6: Consider Community-Based Collaboratives

School systems across the nation are experiencing an unprecedented movement to form collaboratives with institutions in their larger communities to achieve educational reforms aimed at dropout prevention (Barr & Parrett, 1995; Dillick, 1953; Institute for Educational Leadership, 1986; Jones, 1992; Levine, 1988; McMullan, 1987; Upton, 1984). Education stakeholders generally recognize that only through collaboration—schools working with other institutions to address common areas of concern—can the multitude of student and school needs be addressed (Fantini, 1985; Jones, 1992; Passow, 1985). One example is the community-based organization (CBO).

The growth of school-CBO collaboratives is associated with the development of broader community involvement in education. This involvement has been ignited by the growing importance of education (Boyer, 1983) and diminishing resources for schools (Fantini, 1985), coupled with the school dropout problem (Jones, 1992; Levin, 1985).

One such CBO is the New York City Attendance Improvement Dropout Prevention (AIDP) program. One of the major goals of the AIDP program is to engage schools in collaborative initiatives with CBOs to prevent students from dropping out of school (Jones, 1992). The AIDP program was launched in 29 New York City middle schools with a $13 million joint budget allocation from the New York state legislature, the New York City mayor's office, and the New York City Central Board of Education. The types of services provided to the students enrolled in the AIDP program at each of the schools include

■ Additional guidance and counseling services in the form of individual and group counseling sessions

■ Additional health services such as diagnostic screening of targeted students in physical, psychological, and educational areas and referral for appropriate follow-up

■ Attendance outreach to ensure the carrying out of home visits and parent conferences between teachers and parents whose children were enrolled in the program

■ Alternative educational activities that incorporated basic skills instruction with individualized attention and after-school academic and social support programming (Jones, 1992, p. 499)

Strategy 7: Establish a Case Management Intervention System

Case management intervention has been used as a tool to reduce the rate of high school dropouts. The Albany City School District, in conjunction with the State University of New York at Albany (SUNYA), established such a program. The program consists of four components: academic assistance, social services, employment services, and a computerized database resource file (Gaudette & Niccoli, 1992).

The academic assistance component evaluates, assists, and monitors students' academic progress. Working in collaboration with teachers and school counselors, the program coordinator identifies areas for remediation, and an individual tutorial regimen is established. At-risk students are assigned a tutor for one-on-one academic instruction. The tutors are students from the teacher training program at SUNYA. The tutors provide at-risk students with basic instruction in core subjects, individualized attention in elective courses, encouragement, and positive reinforcement.

The social services component addresses the social pressures that interfere with students' educational goals. This component draws on Community Service Project interns from SUNYA. Pairing at-risk students with SUNYA preservice teachers produces mentoring relationships. Consequently, at-risk students receive social skill development, crisis resolution techniques, and, when needed, referrals to community agencies.

employment services component connects at-risk students
)rt- and long-term employment services. This is provided
through partnerships with the School and Business Alliance (SABA)
and the Youth Internship Program (YIP), sponsored by Hudson Valley
Community College. SABA provides employment-related workshops
and supervised work experiences designed to build employment skills
and work history. YIP provides employment workshops, internships
with local businesses, and connections to postsecondary education
through Hudson Valley Community College.

Case management intervention staff develop a computerized database resource file. The file contains descriptions of community resources, including referral criteria and services available. Such a database enables the program coordinator to match students' needs with
appropriate community services (Gaudette & Niccoli, 1992).

Strategy 8: Create a Mentoring Network

Matching retirees with at-risk students is a cost-effective way to
provide potential dropouts with adult role models. Several such mentoring programs exist (Freedman, 1989, 1994; Freedman & Jaffe,
1993). For example, the Teaching-Learning Communities (T-LC)
Mentoring Program in Ann Arbor, Michigan, and other cities assigns
retired adults as mentors and tutors to junior and senior high school
students who are at risk of dropping out. The program stresses the
arts, career awareness, personal goal setting, consistent school attendance, and educational excellence.

School Volunteers for Boston (SVB)—which is similar to programs operating in such urban areas as Los Angeles, Dallas, New
York, and San Francisco—places retired adult mentors in classrooms
and after-school programs to tutor at-risk students in basic reading
and mathematics and to participate in a variety of mentoring activities.
The Teenage Parent Alternative Program (TAPA) in Lincoln, Michigan,
pairs foster grandparents with teenage parents. The elder mentors
help teach the young mothers about parenting and health care for their
child, and also watch the child while the mother is in class (Freedman
& Jaffe, 1993).

Two other programs that link adult mentors with at-risk students
are People Against Losing Students (PALS) and Parents Reaching Out
(PRO) in Tatum, Texas. The two programs together have three main
thrusts: career awareness, academics, and parenting. Students in the

programs get extra counseling and help from community volunteers and school personnel with career awareness, achieving class objectives, and the skills required to rear children.

Strategy 9: Establish a School Within a School

School-within-a-school (SWS) initiatives typically are locally funded programs of instruction in basic skills, career guidance, and counseling support to meet the needs of at-risk junior and senior high school students. The SWS program calls for teachers to work as a team across academic disciplines to meet to plan curriculum, the budget, in-house discipline, and enrichment activities. Students are drawn primarily from the larger school's attendance area and from populations that traditionally do poorly in high school and are underrepresented in college: African American, Hispanic, and other nonwhite students.

SWS program guidelines outline services that address academic, personal and social, and vocational growth of SWS students. SWS courses generally have the same objectives as the regular school curriculum. The same textbooks and evaluation measures are used for SWS classes. The primary modifications to the regular educational program are teaching strategies and the degree of individualization allowed by smaller class sizes. Social and emotional growth, an important goal of SWS programs, is promoted through cooperative learning, cross-age mentoring, traditional mentoring, life skills classes, service learning projects, SWS home rooms, and student-developed field trips, orientations, graduation ceremonies, and awards ceremonies (Gordon, 1993).

Ten elements that make SWS programs successful are:

1. *Application and assessment process.* Students must apply to SWS, explaining why they want to participate. Once admitted, their progress is monitored frequently using a variety of assessment measures.

2. *Low student-teacher ratio.* SWS classes are maintained at a student-teacher ratio of 15 to 1 maximum. The use of community volunteers helps to lower the ratio even more.

3. *Positive physical and mental environment.* SWS programs strive for library-like surroundings, with study carrels and large tables, decorated with plants and motivational posters on the walls.

4. *Appropriate curriculum.* The SWS curriculum parallels that used in the regular school program. Modifications in the curriculum and teaching methods are made so that the full spectrum of students' learning styles is accommodated.

5. *Structured environment.* Well-articulated policies and procedures foster a meaningful, purposeful classroom atmosphere. Students make a commitment to the SWS program by signing contracts.

6. *Attendance incentives.* Daily attendance is mandatory. Parents are encouraged to call when students are absent. Teachers call parents when students are absent even 1 day.

7. *Connections with counselors.* To help keep students on track, counselors meet with them weekly to discuss the program, their progress, and peer and adult relationships.

8. *Cooperation with other teachers.* SWS faculty monitor and encourage students' progress in other classes through periodic reports and communication with other teachers.

9. *Parent conferences.* Conferences with parents are scheduled as needed. SWS faculty keep parents well informed concerning participants' progress.

10. *Community relations.* Successful SWS programs build bridges of support. Students tell their friends. Parents lend their praise. Businesses invite students for tours of their facilities. Volunteers experience the benefits of a successful program firsthand (Nevares, 1992).

Strategy 10: Use State-Legislated
Negative-Sanction Policies

A radically different strategy is to invoke negative sanctions on the potential dropout (Toby & Armor, 1992). For example, in Wisconsin, if a child fails to attend school regularly, the state reduces benefits to the student's family on welfare. The sanction is designed to hold parents accountable for their children's attendance pattern. In West Virginia, a similar sanction policy began with a program that aims to decrease the dropout rate in that state by revoking the driver's license of any minor student who drops out of high school before graduation.

The West Virginia "no school, no drive" law attracted considerable attention across the nation. Now Arkansas, Florida, Kentucky, Louisiana, Mississippi, Tennessee, and other states have passed similar laws that require good school attendance records for new licensees and revoke the existing licenses of dropouts or those with poor attendance records who are under 18 (Toby & Armor, 1992).

Making sure that by the year 2000 and beyond, 90% of the students graduate from high school is not an impossible charge. We have many strategies available to us. Internet search engines can help administrators, teachers, and parents locate examples of prevention programs for their communities and schools. The information in Chapter 1 on assisting children in their readiness for school cannot be overlooked in the maintenance of dropout prevention beyond 2000.

References

Acheson, K. A., & Gall, M. D. (1998). *Techniques in the clinical supervision of teachers* (4th ed.). White Plains, NY: Longman.

Alexander, K., Natriello, G., & Pallas, A. (1985). For whom the bell tolls: The impact of dropping out on cognitive performance. *American Sociological Review, 50,* 409-420.

Altman, N. (1995). *The analyst in the inner city: Race, class, and culture through a psychoanalytic lens.* Hillsdale, NJ: Analytic.

Archer, E., Weinbaum, S., & Montesano, P. (1989). *Partnerships for learning: School completion and employment preparation in the high school academies.* New York: Academy for Educational Development.

Arhar, J. M. (1992, Spring). Enhancing students' feelings of school membership: What principals can do. *Schools in the Middle,* pp. 12-16.

Baldwin, B., Moffett, M. R., & Lane, K. (1992). The high school dropout: Antecedents and alternatives. *Journal of School Leadership, 2,* 355-362.

Barr, R. D., & Parrett, W. H. (1995). *Hope at last for at-risk youth.* Needham Heights, MA: Allyn & Bacon.

Bazeli, M. J., & Heintz, J. (1997). *Technology across the curriculum: Activities and ideas.* Englewood, CO: Libraries Unlimited.

Boyer, E. (1983). *High school: A report on secondary education in America.* New York: Harper & Row.

Bucci, J. A., & Reitzammer, A. F. (1992). Teachers make a critical difference in dropout prevention. *The Educational Forum, 57,* 63-70.

Bureau of the Census, Economics and Statistics Administration. (1991a). *1990 census profile: Race and Hispanic origin* (No. 2). Washington, DC: Government Printing Office.

Bureau of the Census. (1991b). *Statistical abstract of the United States, 1991.* Washington, DC: Government Printing Office.

Burnett, G. (1992). *Career academies: Educating urban students for career success* (Report No. EDO-UD-92-7). New York: ERIC Clearinghouse on Urban Education, Teachers College, Columbia University. (ERIC Document Reproduction Service No. ED 355 311)

Carbo, M. (1984). You can identify reading styles . . . and then design a super reading program. *Early Years, 68*(6), 80-83.

Carbo, M. (1987a). Deprogramming reading failure: Giving unequal learners an equal chance. *Phi Delta Kappan, 45*(2) 197-202.

Carbo, M. (1987b, October). Matching reading styles: Correcting ineffective instruction. *Educational Leadership,* pp. 55-62.

Carnegie Foundation for the Advancement of Teaching. (1988). *An imperiled generation: Saving urban schools.* Lawrenceville, NJ: Princeton University Press.

Clayton, D. E. (1991). *Testimony on federal education policy for the 102nd Congress.* Washington, DC: United States Senate, Committee on Labor and Human Resources.

Council of the Great City Schools. (1992). *Urban schools of America.* Washington, DC: Author.

Dayton, C., Weisberg, A., & Stern, D. (1989). *California partnership academies: 1987-88 evaluation report* (Policy paper no. PP 89-9-1). Berkeley: University of California, Policy Analysis for California Education.

Dillick, S. (1953). *Community organization for neighborhood development: Past and present.* New York: William Morrow.

Dunn, R., & Dunn, K. (1992a). *Teaching elementary students through their individual learning styles: Practical approaches for grades 3-6.* Needham Heights, MA: Allyn & Bacon.

Dunn, R., & Dunn, K. (1992b). *Teaching secondary students through their individual learning styles: Practical approaches for grades 7-12.* Needham Heights, MA: Allyn & Bacon.

Fantini, M. (1985). Stages of linking schools and nonschool learning environments. In M. Fantini & R. Sinclair (Eds.), *Education in school and nonschool settings* (pp. 46-63). Chicago: University of Chicago Press.

Freedman, M. (1989). *Partners in growth.* Philadelphia: Public/Private Ventures.

Freedman, M. (1994). *From the goodness of our hearts: The emergence of mentoring programs for vulnerable youth.* New York: McGraw-Hill.

Freedman, M., & Jaffe, N. (1993). Elder mentors: Giving schools a hand. *NASSP Bulletin, 76*(549), 22-28.

Gardner, H. (1985). *Frames of mind.* New York: Basic Books.

Gaudette, J., & Niccoli, K. (1992). Case management as an educational intervention: Implications for reducing high school dropouts. *Catalyst, 21*(2), 10-13.

Good, T. (1987). Two decades of research on teacher expectations: Findings and future directions. *Journal of Teacher Education, 38,* 32-47.

Gordon, R. (1993). The school within a school program. *ERS Spectrum, 11*(1), 27-30.

Hengstler, D. D., Reichard, D. J., Uhl, N. P., & Goldman, B. A. (1981). *Prediction of academic success with the Myers-Briggs Type Indicator.* (ERIC Document Reproduction Service No. ED205 129)

Hodgkinson, J. L. (1992). *A demographic look at tomorrow.* Washington, DC: Institute for Educational Leadership.

Hodgkinson, J. L. (1996). *Predicting demographics in the nation's schools.* Washington, DC: Institute for Educational Leadership.

Institute for Educational Leadership. (1986). *School dropouts: Everybody's problem.* Washington, DC: Author.

Jones, B. A. (1992). Collaboration: The case for indigenous community-based organization support of dropout prevention programming and implementation. *Journal of Negro Education, 61*(4), 496-508.

Jung, C. G. (1923). *Psychological types.* New York: Harcourt Brace.

Kiersey, D., & Bates, M. (1978). *Please understand me: Character and temperament types.* Del Mar, CA: Prometheus Nemesis.

Kreitzer, A. E., Madaus, G. F., & Haney, N. (1989). Competency testing and dropouts. In L. Weis, E. Farrar, & H. G. Petrie (Eds.),

Dropouts from school: Issues, dilemmas, and solutions (pp. 129-152). Albany: State University of New York Press.

Lawrence, G. (1979). *People types and tiger stripes.* Gainesville, FL: Center for Application of Psychological Type.

Lehr, J. B., & Harris, H. W. (1991). *At-risk, low achieving students in the classroom.* Washington, DC: National Education Association.

Levin, H. (1972). *The costs of the nation of inadequate education.* Washington, DC: Government Printing Office.

Levin, H. (1985). *The educationally disadvantaged: A national crisis.* Philadelphia: Public/Private Ventures.

Levine, M. (1988). *American business and the public schools: Case studies of corporate involvement in public education.* New York: Teachers College Press.

Lincoln, C. A., & Higgins, N. M. (1991). Making schools work for all children. *Principal, 70*(3), 6-9.

Mann, D. (1986). Can we help dropouts: Thinking about the undoable. In G. Natriello (Ed.), *School dropouts: Patterns and policies.* New York: Teachers College Press.

Manning, M. L., & Baruth, L. (1995). *Students at risk.* Needham Heights, MA: Allyn & Bacon.

Maxwell, M. (1981). *Improving student learning skills.* San Francisco: Jossey-Bass.

McCaulley, M. H. (1981). Jung's theory of psychological types and the Myers-Briggs Type Indicator. In P. Reynolds (Ed.), *Advances in personality assessment* (Vol. 5, pp. 294-352). San Francisco: Jossey-Bass.

McCaulley, M. H., & Natter, F. L. (1974). Psychological type differences in education. In F. L. Natter & S. A. Rollin (Eds.), *The Governor's Task Force On Disruptive Youth: Phase II report* (pp. 92-112). Gainesville, FL: Center for Application of Psychological Type.

McDill, E., Natriello, G., & Pallas, A. (1985). Raising standards and retaining students: The impact of the reform recommendations of potential dropouts. *Review of Educational Research, 55,* 415-433.

McMullan, B. (1987). *Allies in education: Schools and business working together for at-risk youth.* Philadelphia: Public/Private Ventures.

McNeal, R. B. (1995). Extracurricular activities and high school dropouts. *Sociology of Education, 68,* 62-81.

Mott, F. L., & Marsigolio, W. (1985). Early childbearing and the completion of high school. *Family Planning Perspectives, 17,* 234-237.

Myers-Briggs, I. (1962). *The Myers-Briggs Type Indicator: Manual.* Palo Alto, CA: Consulting Psychologists Press.

Meyers-Briggs, I. (1975). *The Myers-Briggs Type Indicator: Manual* (rev. ed.). Palo Alto, CA: Consulting Psychologists Press.

National Center for Education Statistics. (1996). *Annual digest of education statistics.* Washington, DC: Department of Education, Office of Educational Research Improvement.

Natriello, G., McDill, E. L., & Pallas, A. M. (1990). *Schooling disadvantaged children: Racing against catastrophe.* New York: Teachers College Press.

Nevares, L. (1992). Credit where credit is due. *The Executive Educator, 12*(12), 50-53.

Nisbet, J., Ruble, V., & Schurr, K. T. (1981, April). *Predictors of academic success with the Myers-Briggs Type Indicator.* Paper presented at the 21st annual forum of the Association for Institutional Research, Minneapolis, MN. (ERIC Document Reproduction Service No. ED 205 129)

Passow, A. H. (1985). Combined efforts: Models for nonschool settings for learning. In M. Fantini & R. Sinclair (Eds.), *Education in school and nonschool settings* (pp. 64-78). Chicago: University of Chicago Press.

Population Reference Bureau. (1995). *The American population in the 21st century.* Washington, DC: Government Printing Office.

Praport, H. (1993). Reducing high school attrition: Group counseling can help. *The School Counselor, 40,* 309-311.

Robyak, J. E., & Patton, M. J. (1977). The effectiveness of a study skill course for students of different personality types. *Journal of Counseling Psychology, 24*(3), 200-207.

Ruff, T. P. (1993, May). Middle school students at risk: What do we do with the most vulnerable children in American education? *Middle School Journal,* pp. 10-12.

Rumberger, R. (1987). High school dropouts: A review of issues and evidence. *Review of Educational Research, 57,* 101-121.

Stern, D., Raby, M., & Dayton, C. (1992). *Career academies: Partnerships for reconstructing American high schools.* San Francisco: Jossey-Bass.

Toby, J., & Armor, D. J. (1992). Carrots or sticks for high school dropouts. *Public Interest, 106,* 76-90.

Upton, J. (1984). Community organizations: Strategies for influencing public policy. *Urban Education, 19*(3), 201-225.

Van, B. (1992). The MBTI: Implications for retention. *Journal of Developmental Education, 16*(1), 20-23.

VanderMolen, J. A., & Nolan, R. R. (1993). Agenda for at-risk kids. *American School Board Journal, 180*(1), 40-41.

Wehlage, G. G., Rutter, R. A., Smith, G. A., Lesko, N., & Fernandez, R. R. (1989). *Reducing the risk: Schools as communities of support.* New York: Falmer.

CHAPTER 3

Every Student Competent

*By the year 2000, all students will leave grades 4, 8,
and 12 having demonstrated competency over challenging subject matter including English, mathematics,
science, foreign languages, civics and government,
economics, arts, history, and geography; and every
school in America will ensure that all students learn
to use their minds well, so they may be prepared for
responsible citizenship, further learning, and productive employment in our Nation's modern economy.*
(Goals 2000: Educate America Act of 1994)

Although each of the eight national education goals is important,
increasing student achievement in the core subject areas—English,
mathematics, science, foreign languages, civics and government, economics, arts, history, and geography—will be the ultimate test of successful education reform. The third goal states that upon completion
of grades 4, 8 and 12, all students will demonstrate competency in
challenging subject matter in the aforementioned subject areas and
learn to use their minds well.

Applying Research to Practice:
Developing an Action Plan

To achieve major improvements in student achievement will require fundamental changes in the expectations schools set for all

Box 3.1. What the Research Says

◆ Since 1970, the National Assessment of Educational Progress (NAEP) tests have been used to assess students' performance in the core subject areas annually. NAEP is the only nationally representative continuing assessment that measures what students know and are able to do in the core subject areas (Department of Education, 1994).

◆ The data suggest that student outcomes in American education are little better—and in some cases worse—than they were 25 years ago. NAEP reports that only one third of 12th graders are able to perform rigorous reading passages. The average reading level of black 17-year-olds is about 4 years behind that of white students (Department of Education, 1994).

◆ Differences between white and Hispanic reading scores on the NAEP have been declining consistently since 1975 (Bracey, 1996).

◆ The gap between white and Hispanic mathematics scores on the NAEP has been declining since 1973 (Bracey, 1996).

◆ "Currently 30% of SAT-takers are minorities, 52% are women, 83% have attended public schools, and 41% report an annual family income of $40,000 or less" (Bracey, 1996, p. 132).

◆ Merely 11% of secondary students demonstrate a good understanding of history. The general standards of American schools compare unfavorably with those of other industrialized nations (Department of Education, 1994).

◆ NAEP data suggest that students are not learning how to think. In other words, although student learning of facts and basic skills has improved slightly in some subject areas over the past two decades, the development of more advanced reasoning abilities has declined (Department of Education, 1994).

students, the types of courses schools offer, the way teachers are trained (see Chapter 4), and the way subject matter is taught. Leaders should consider recent movements such as critical thinking and constructivism that offer real promise for improving the achievement of all students in the core subject areas. In addition, these instructional designs are well suited to technological intervention within the class-room (McManus & Aiken, 1995).

Strategy 1: Teach Critical Thinking

The Center for Critical Thinking (1997) provides an excellent treatise on critical thinking applied to instruction. Critical thinking shifts classroom design from a model that largely ignores thinking to one that renders it pervasive and necessary. Critical teaching views content as something alive only in minds, modes of thinking driven by questions, existing in textbooks only to be regenerated in the minds of students.

Once we understand content as inseparable from the thinking that generates, organizes, analyzes, synthesizes, evaluates, and transforms it, we recognize that content cannot in principle ever be "completed" because thinking is never completed. To understand content, there-fore, is to understand its implications. But to understand its implica-tions, one must understand that those implications in turn have fur-ther implications, and hence must be thoughtfully explored.

The problem with didactic teaching is that content is inadvertently treated as static, as virtually "dead." Content is treated as something to be mimicked, to be repeated back, to be parroted. And because students only rarely process content deeply when they play the role of passive listeners in lecture-centered instruction, little is learned in the long term. Furthermore, because students are taught content in a way that renders them unlikely to think it through, their minds retreat into rote memorization, abandoning any attempt to grasp the logic of what they are committing to memory.

Those who teach critically emphasize that only those who can "think" through content truly learn it. Content "dies" when one tries to learn it mechanically. Content has to take root in the thinking of students and, when properly learned, transforms the way they think. Hence, when students study a subject in a critical way, they take pos-session of a new mode to thinking that, so internalized, generates new thoughts, understandings, and beliefs. Their thinking, now driven by a set of new questions, becomes an instrument of insight and a new point of view.

History texts become, in the minds of students thinking critically, a stimulus to historical thinking. Geography texts are internalized as geographical thinking. Mathematical content is transformed into mathematical thinking. As a result of being taught to think critically, students study biology and become biological thinkers. They study sociology and begin to notice the permissions, injunctions, and taboos of the groups in which they participate. They study literature and begin to notice the way in which all humans tend to define their lives in the stories they tell. They study economics and begin to notice how much of their behavior is intertwined with economic forces and needs.

There are ways, indeed almost an unlimited number, to stimulate critical thinking at every educational level and in every teaching setting. When considering technology for this stimulation, the World Wide Web (WWW) is important to instructional design; it contains three keys to educational value: hypertext, the delivery of multimedia, and true interactivity (Starr, 1997). These values are operant and alive in the classroom through such applications as graphics, sound, and video, which bring to life world events, museum tours, library visits, world visits, and up-to-date weather maps. Through these WWW mechanisms, a constructivist instructional model advances higher-level instruction, such as problem solving and increased learner control. The WWW becomes a necessary tool for student-centered discovery and research (Quinlan, 1997). Of course, it can also be used for lower-level drill and practice.

At every level and in all subjects, students need to learn how to ask questions precisely, define contexts and purposes, pursue relevant information, analyze key concepts, derive sound inferences, generate good reasons, recognize questionable assumptions, trace important implications, and think empathetically within different points of view. The WWW enables learners and teachers in each area by providing information for good reasoners to figure things out. Critical thinking may be a key organizing concept for all educational reform (Foundation for Critical Thinking, 1997).

Strategy 2: Consider Constructivism

Constructivism may be the most significant recent trend in education relative to the dynamic relationship between how teachers teach and how children learn (Marzano, 1992; McClelland, Marsh, & Podemski, 1994). One foundational premise of constructivism is that children actively construct their knowledge, rather than simply absorbing ideas spoken to them by teachers. For example, Jean Piaget (1970) and his coworkers proposed that children make sense in ways very different from adults, and that they learn through the process of trying to make things happen, trying to manipulate their environment. Theories such as these, which assert that "people are not recorders of information, but builders of knowledge structures" (Resnick & Klopfer, 1989, p. 4), have been grouped under the heading of *constructivism*. Thus, students are ultimately responsible for their own learning within a learning atmosphere in which teachers value student thinking, initiate lessons that foster cooperative learning, provide opportunities for students to be exposed to interdisciplinary curriculum, structure learning around primary concepts, and facilitate authentic assessment of student understanding.

In constructivist theory, it is assumed that learners have to construct their own knowledge—individually and collectively. Each learner has a repertoire of conceptions and skills with which she or he must construct knowledge to solve problems presented by the environment. The role of the teacher and other learners is to provide the setting, pose the challenges, and offer the support that will encourage cognitive construction. Because students lack the experience of experts in the field, teachers bear a great responsibility for guiding student activity, modeling behavior, and providing examples that will transform student group discussions into meaningful communication about subject matter.

Constructivism emphasizes the processes by which children create and develop their ideas. Applications lie in creating curricula that not only match but also challenge children's understanding, fostering further growth and development of the mind (Strommen & Lincoln, 1992). Furthermore, when children collaborate in cooperative learning groups, they share the process of constructing their ideas with others. This collective effort provides the opportunity for children to reflect on and elaborate not only their own ideas but also those of their peers. With improvement of and access to the WWW, the children's cooperative classroom becomes the world. In this cooperative learning setting, children view their peers as resources rather than as competitors. A feeling of teamwork ensues. These processes have resulted in substantial advances in student learning (Beilin & Pufall, 1992; Halford, 1993; Presseisen, 1986; Resnick & Klopfer, 1989; Schunk & Zimmerman, 1994; Steffe & Gale, 1995).

Constructivism is serving as the basis for many of the current reforms in several subject matter disciplines. The National Council of Teachers of Mathematics (NCTM; 1989) published *Curriculum and*

Evaluation Standards for School Mathematics, which calls for mathematics classrooms where problem solving, concept development, and the construction of learner-generated solutions and algorithms are stressed rather than drill and practice on correct procedures and facts to get the "right" answer. The National Committee on Science Education Standards and Assessment (1996) similarly issued *National Science Education Standards,* which calls for science education reform based on experimentation and learner-generated inquiry, investigations, hypotheses, and models. The National Council of Teachers of English (NCTE) has called for emergent literacy as an important thrust in language arts reform. Interdisciplinary curricula is the theme of social studies reform being advocated by the National Council of Social Studies.

Principles of Constructivist Pedagogy

Jacqueline Brooks and Martin Brooks (1993) provide a detailed description of constructivist classroom practice and its theoretical underpinnings in their book, *The Case for Constructivist Classrooms.* They provide five principles of constructivist pedagogy: (1) posing problems of emerging relevance to learners; (2) structuring learning around "big ideas" or primary concepts; (3) seeking and valuing students' points of view; (4) adapting curriculum to address students' suppositions; and (5) assessing student learning in the context of teaching.

Principle 1. Posing Problems of Emerging Relevance to Students. Relevance does not have to be preexisting for the student. Not all students come to the classroom interested in learning. Relevance can emerge through teacher mediation.

Principle 2. Structuring Learning Around Primary Concepts. When designing curriculum, constructivist teachers organize information around conceptual clusters of problems, questions, and discrepant situations because students are most engaged when problems and ideas are presented holistically rather than in separate, isolated parts. Much of traditional education breaks wholes into parts and then focuses separately on each part, but many students are unable to build concepts and skills from parts to wholes.

Principle 3. Seeking and Valuing Students' Points of View. Students' points of view are avenues into their reasoning. Awareness of students' points of view helps teachers challenge students, making school experiences both contextual and meaningful. Teachers who operate without awareness of their students' points of view often doom students to dull, irrelevant experiences, and even failure.

Principle 4. Adapting Curriculum to Address Students' Suppositions. Teacher mediation is a key factor in adapting curriculum to address students' suppositions. The teacher can abstract student learning or help build students' own bridges from present understandings to new, more complex understandings. If suppositions are not explicitly addressed, most students will find lessons devoid of meaning, regardless of how charismatic the teacher or attractive the materials used. Although it is the teacher who structures the opportunity, it is the students' own reflective abstractions that create the new understanding.

Principle 5. Assessing Student Learning in the Context of Teaching. Multiple choice, norm-referenced tests are structured to determine whether students know information related to a particular body of knowledge. The overarching question posed by such activities is: What do you know? Authentic assessment focuses on analytical thinking and performance, whereas norm-referenced, standardized tests focus on low-level rote skills.

Become a Constructivist Teacher

Brooks and Brooks (1993) provide the following set of descriptors of constructivist teaching behaviors that they feel teachers can use to experiment with the approach. The set of descriptors describes teachers as facilitators of learning and empowerers of students to construct their own understandings of content, not simply as providers of information and managers of behavior.

1. *Constructivist teachers encourage and accept student autonomy and initiative.* Autonomy and initiative cause students' pursuit of connections among concepts. Students who formulate questions and then go on to answer and analyze them are taking responsibility for their own learning and become problem solvers as well as problem finders.

2. *Constructivist teachers use raw data and primary sources, along with manipulatives and interactive and physical materials.* In the

constructivist approach to teaching, learning becomes the result of research related to real problems. For example, students can be assigned to read historical accounts of the effects of social policies of the early 1980s on the economic profile of the African American population. Or students can be taught to read the census reports and encouraged to generate their own inferences about social policies. The latter approach allows students to construct their own understandings of the issues.

3. *When framing tasks, constructivist teachers use cognitive terminology such as "classify," "analyze," "predict," and "create."* Formulating tasks around cognitive activities such as analysis, interpretation, classification, and prediction—and explicitly using those terms with students—fosters the construction of new understandings about content.

4. *Constructivist teachers allow student responses to drive lessons, shift instructional strategies, and alter content.* This does not mean that students' interest or lack of interest in a topic determines whether the topic is taught or that whole sections of the curriculum will be eliminated. It does mean that constructivist teachers will capitalize on "teachable moments" throughout the school year. These are moments when the students' interest, knowledge, and enthusiasm intersect and transcend a particular lesson. For example, the Persian Gulf War may have provoked student initiated discussion during that time period.

5. *Constructivist teachers inquire about students' understandings of concepts before sharing their own understandings of those concepts.* When teachers share their ideas before students have an opportunity to formulate their own, students' examination of their own ideas is eliminated. In such environments, most students will stop thinking about the concept and wait for the teacher to provide the "correct answer." Consequently, students are prevented from constructing their own ideas and theories.

6. *Constructivist teachers encourage students to engage in dialogue, both with the teacher and with one another.* One way that students change or reinforce their ideas and theories is through social discourse. Students are empowered when they have an opportunity to

present their own ideas and hear and reflect on the ideas of others. This process helps students construct new understandings or reflect on their existing ones. According to Robert Slavin (1990), student-to-student dialogue is the foundation on which cooperative learning is based.

7. *Constructivist teachers encourage student inquiry by asking thoughtful, open-ended questions and encouraging students to ask questions of each other.* Complex, thoughtful questions that have more than one response challenge students to delve into issues deeply and broadly and to form their own understandings of events and phenomena.

8. *Constructivist teachers seek elaboration of students' initial responses.* Students' initial responses about issues are not necessarily their final thoughts nor their best thoughts on a topic. Through elaboration of initial responses, students frequently reconceptualize and assess their own errors and, in the process, construct their own understandings of issues, concepts, and theories.

9. *Constructivist teachers engage students in experiences that might engender contradictions to their initial hypotheses and then encourage discussion.* Cognitive growth occurs when an individual reformulates a current perspective. Students at all levels formulate and refine ideas about phenomena and then tenaciously hold onto these ideas as eternal truths. Even when confronted with authoritative evidence that challenges their views, students generally adhere to their original ideas. When teachers provide experiences that might engender contradictions, the framework for students' original ideas weaken, causing them to rethink their perspectives and formulate new understandings.

10. *Constructivist teachers allow time after posing questions.* In most classrooms, some students are not prepared to respond to questions or other stimuli immediately. They require more time to process information. Teachers who require immediate responses prevent these students from thinking through theories and concepts thoroughly, forcing them to become spectators. These students quickly learn that there is no point in mentally engaging in teacher-posed questions.

11. *Constructivist teachers provide time for students to construct relationships and create metaphors.* Constructivist teachers structure and mediate classroom activities and provide the necessary time and materials for learning to occur, which causes students to construct patterns, relationships among concepts and theories for themselves. Constructivist teachers also encourage the use of metaphor as a way to facilitate learning. Metaphors help students understand complex issues in a holistic way and ruminate mentally with the parts of the whole to determine whether the metaphor works.

12. *Constructivist teachers nurture students' natural curiosity through frequent use of the learning cycle model.* The learning cycle model has been used in science education for some time. The best description of the model is by Atkin and Karplus (1962). The model describes curriculum development and instruction as a three-step cycle: discovery, concept introduction, and concept application. First, the teacher provides an open-ended opportunity for students to interact with purposefully selected materials. This step is designed to generate student questions and hypotheses from working with the materials (discovery). Next, the teacher provides lessons aimed at focusing students' questions, providing related and new vocabulary, framing with students their laboratory experiences, and such (concept introduction). Finally, students engage in one or more interactions of the discovery-concept introduction sequence. Students work on new problems with the potential for evoking a reflective, new look at the concepts studied previously (concept application).

The 12 descriptors of constructivist teaching highlight practices that help students construct their own understandings of challenging subject-matter content. These descriptors can serve as guidelines for interpreting what it means to become a constructivist teacher. For specific examples of how to implement each of the descriptors, see Brooks and Brooks (1993).

Strategy 3: Investigate Current Restructuring Initiatives

Although school reform has been ubiquitous for the past century, little of significance has changed (Cuban, 1988, 1990). Since the advent of compulsory education, neither the technology nor the core beliefs of schooling has changed substantively (Timar, 1989). Our restructuring efforts need to be based on a set of core principles that help participating schools identify with ideas larger than the individual, the classroom, the school, or the community (Lieberman, 1992; Lieberman & Miller, 1990). Recent initiatives that begin to address these ideas include six national restructuring efforts: the Coalition of Essential Schools, Success for All, the Comer School development model, the Paideia program, outcomes-based education, and electronic communities (Challenge Grants for Technology in Education). Although the ways of implementing these core beliefs may differ, the principles provide a framework for school restructuring.

Coalition of Essential Schools

The Coalition of Essential Schools, a project intended to restructure the nature of secondary schooling, forms its core principles from the work of Theodore Sizer (1984, 1992, 1997), who serves as chair of the coalition. Since its formation in 1985, the Coalition of Essential Schools has included more than 250 schools in 35 states and two Canadian provinces. Schools that have projects under way are reporting encouraging results, especially in urban settings, in some of the simple measures, including increased attendance, decreased dropout rates, higher test scores, and fewer discipline problems (Sizer, 1992).

The mission of coalition-member schools is to create an intellectual environment in which instruction is personalized, and students are responsible for their own learning. The goal is that each student who graduates from high school will have the ability to think, inquire, and reason. Although coalition-member schools have no blueprint to go by, all subscribe to a set of nine core principles (Sizer, 1984, 1992, 1997).

1. *Personalized instruction.* Teaching and learning should be personalized, with teachers and principals responsible for what is studied, how time is spent, and what materials and pedagogues are used. The teacher load should not exceed 80 students. For the most part, coalition schools have restructured the school day so they can teach fewer students for longer periods of time. For example, 80 students might take part in a common core program taught by four teachers for 4 hours each day. Curriculum and instruction in the core are interdisciplinary, covering language arts, mathematics, social science, and science. One teacher assumes responsibility for each area of the

curriculum, and teachers have complete discretion over how much time to devote to the teaching of each subject. Built into each teacher's schedule is an hour of team planning. Such a configuration occurs schoolwide or in a school-within-a-school structure.

2. *Student as worker, teacher as coach.* The governing metaphor of the school should be student as worker, not teacher as deliverer of instructional services. Working in a coalition school requires a radical change in the way teachers think of themselves. Instead of being intellectual authorities standing in front of a class telling, explaining, clarifying, and helping students understand what they know, teachers act as coaches and facilitators who guide and prod their students, who, in turn, are responsible for identifying a problem, developing hypotheses, reasoning, and drawing their own conclusions. Just as the coach of an athletic team doesn't perform for the player, the teacher can't perform for the student. The student is an active participant in the learning situation. Sizer (1992) asserts that students don't learn well when they are passive spectators in the classroom. They need a clear goal that they are expected to reach by actively asking questions, finding solutions, and demonstrating their knowledge.

3. *A "thinking" school.* The school should focus on helping adolescents learn to use their minds well. It is a core principle that reminds teachers that all courses for all students should be designed to maximize the use of higher-order thinking skills. The idea, Sizer (1992) asserts, is to get a student to function effectively in a learning environment that requires intellectual rigor and creativity.

4. *Less is more.* Each student should master a limited number of essential skills and areas of knowledge. The word *essential* in the coalition's name means determining what is essential in the curriculum. Observers of coalition schools are immediately struck by the apparent lack of course electives. When a school offers too many electives, essential courses can be diminished. When a single course is overloaded with content, material tends to be covered, not learned. And because teachers in coalition schools are expected to teach across disciplines, offering a proliferation of courses could result in scheduling problems and pedagogical confusion. Sizer (1992) asserts that the more com-

plicated a school's program is, the less likely that serious intellectual learning will take place.

5. *Generalists first, specialists second.* The principal and teachers should perceive themselves as generalists first and specialists second. Unlike most high schools, teachers in coalition schools are committed to integrating curricula across disciplines and to combining classes as often as possible. Coalition teachers think of themselves as generalists who can teach a broad range of subjects rather than as experts in a given field. This means not only that teachers teach across disciplines, but also that they approach their disciplines as generalists; in other words, that they find interesting ways to introduce specialized material to a general population (Sizer, 1992).

6. *Diploma by exhibition.* The diploma should be awarded upon successful demonstration of mastery. Coalition members believe that getting the right answer is not all that is important. More important is that students show how they arrive at an answer and articulate the reasoning required to reach the conclusion. This approach is best demonstrated through an exhibition, which can take a variety of forms: an oral presentation, a written report, a rap song, a role-playing skit, a musical rendition, or a portfolio of materials. In coalition schools, there is no such thing as a failing grade. Students are required to complete their work satisfactorily no matter how long it takes. Students keep trying until they have completed the task satisfactorily. The problem experienced by coalition teachers is the number of incompletes on some student's records as they move forward in other classes.

7. *Intellectual education for all.* The school's goals should apply to all students. At coalition schools, there are no college-bound, general, or vocational tracks. All students are expected to reach the same goals in the same course of study. According to Sizer (1992), coalition schools take a Jeffersonian view that, aside from a small percentage of students with profound special needs, every student has a mind; democracy depends on the wise use of that mind. Sizer says that our whole system of government depends on the wisdom of the individual citizen. These sentiments are consistent with Mortimer Adler's (1982) *The Paideia Proposal* and Ernest Boyer's (1995) *The Basic School.*

8. *Tone of expectation, trust, and decency.* The tone of the school should stress unanxious expectation, trust, and decency. Coalition schools build a sense of camaraderie and colleagueship among teachers and students. Teachers and students in coalition schools don't view themselves as being on separate sides of the fence. Such an environment leads to a sense of mutual commitment and responsibility for the achievement of the school's goals.

9. *Budgets that support core principles.* Ultimate administrative and budget targets should allow for student loads per teacher of 80 or fewer, time for team planning, and competitive salaries. Because coalition schools are designed to be realistic models of what all public schools should be, it is important for members to demonstrate that they can achieve the core principles within a reasonable budget. The goal is to operate a coalition school on a budget slightly over 10% of the norm. Because start-up costs are actually higher because of research and development of an essential curriculum, additional funding may be necessary. Funds are typically appropriated by the school district, from grants, or with the help of the Coalition of Essential Schools.

Success for All

Success for All (SFA) is a program designed to bring at-risk students quickly to a level at which they can benefit from a classroom of high quality (Madden, Slavin, Karweit, Dolan, & Wasik, 1991). The program was developed to serve prekindergarten through fifth-grade elementary school students. It was implemented in the 1970s in 29 school districts in 16 states. SFA was developed by educational researchers at Johns Hopkins University to prevent students from falling behind. The program's philosophy is to promote prevention as opposed to dealing with the problem after the fact. The goal of the program is to develop successful learners from the start. Parent involvement is essential to SFA.

The family support team keeps parents up to date on how their children are doing in school, encourages parents to volunteer, and suggests strategies that families might use to resolve issues that affects their children's education. Some requirements are important to make the program work: (1) there must be a strong commitment of resources such as money for new positions, materials, staff development and time; (2) the school must reconceptualize preschool through third grade priorities of curriculum; and (3) full support of the administration and faculty is essential if the model is to be done successfully and effectively.

SFA has several different components:

1. *Reading tutors.* SFA uses certified teachers as one-on-one reading tutors to help students become successful readers. Tutors do not have to create a curriculum: They can use the students' regular language arts and reading curriculum and can focus on areas of special needs. Other than one-on-one instruction, tutors work with the regular reading teachers during the daily 90-minute reading periods. Students with the most difficulty learning to read are the highest priority.

2. *Reading program.* Students are grouped each day. The groups are a mixture of gender but all are on the same reading level. The groups average 15 to 20 students. Each group begins in the same manner. It begins with a story read by the teacher, followed by a discussion of new vocabulary, oral language production and comprehension, and story structure. The reading program builds on students' experiences as they grow, and the students move on to increasingly difficult material. Kindergarten and first grade students focus on basic language development relying on Story Telling and Retelling (STAR), big books, oral and written composition, and Peabody Language Development kits. Next, students read shared stories in which students read books that use a phonetically controlled vocabulary. The program also uses STAR, writing activities, and other elements. At the next level, the district's textbooks are used with cooperative learning strategies to continue students' whole language experiences alongside a nonstructured approach to reading and writing. As a part of the program, students are told to read for 20 minutes each night at home under a parent's supervision.

3. *Eight-week reading assessments.* Students' progress is checked after 8-week periods. The assessments are used to place the students in one-on-one tutoring relationships, to move students to more appropriate reading groups, or to identify students who might benefit from other health or social support interventions.

4. *Preschool and kindergarten.* Many schools have preschool and full-day kindergarten using SFA principles. The program emphasizes academic and nonacademic activities.

5. *Family support team.* Depending on the school's resources, the family support team usually is made up of a social worker, an attendance monitor, and other staff in addition to school staff such as administrators, teachers, Chapter 1 teachers, and an SFA facilitator. The team helps involve parents through frequent contact, recruits parents to be volunteers in the school community, refers families to other services as necessary, and works to coordinate family-level activities with the school's academic program.

6. *Program facilitator.* Each program has a facilitator who works with the principal. The facilitator helps with scheduling and works directly with teachers and tutors. The facilitator often meets with teaching and tutoring staff on a weekly basis.

7. *Teachers and teacher training.* Both regular classroom teachers and the reading tutors are certified in elementary, early childhood, or reading. All professional staff attend a 2-day inservice before the beginning of school, along with 4 days of inservice throughout the school year. The inservice provides a comprehensive set of teaching guides. The content of the inservice varies according to grade level. Tutors spend another day during the year on tutoring strategies and assessment.

8. *Special education.* SFA works with special needs students within the context of the classroom. Tutors, some of whom are special educators, work with individual students.

9. *Advisory committee.* An advisory committee should be made up of the principal, the facilitator, the teacher, and a member of the family support team. The group oversees the program's progress (Department of Education Planning and Evaluation, 1997).

Comer School Development Model

The Comer school development model was created to be used in any kindergarten through grade 12 school; however, the majority of the schools using this model have been elementary and middle schools. The program was designed by James Comer, a child psychiatrist and administrator at the Yale Child Study Center. The most common source for the model is Comer's (1980) book, *School Power: Implications of an Intervention Project.* The project was initially created 20 years ago. The program is based on a strong commitment to expand the role of schools in dealing with the developmental needs of children, particularly disadvantaged children in urban settings. During the 1970s, Comer believed that the effectiveness of schools depends on their ability to meet the mental health and social needs of their children. One way to achieve these goals is for schools to become less isolated from their communities.

The Comer model suggests community participation, particularly by their student's parents. The long-term goal of the program is to improve the academic achievement of students. The program assumes that this goal can be met most effectively by dealing with community involvement and the social needs of the students. Parent participation is strongly encouraged. There are three levels at which this can be accomplished. The first step concerns structuring broad-based activities for a large number of parents. The second step is approximately one parent per professional staff member working in the school as a classroom assistant, tutor, or aide. The third step is a few highly involved parents participating in school governance.

The Comer school development model typically takes a few years to become established in a school, but it can be implemented without large amounts of additional resources such as staff, equipment, or materials. One major requirement is that the school staff and community be committed to the goals and activities of the program. No school staff already involved in the model can claim to have "fully" implemented the model. There must be continuous training and monitoring to support the model regardless of how long it has been implemented. Development program activities for staff and parents initially focus on how to be an effective member of school governance and mental health teams. The child study group at Yale does the initial training, but it does encourage the school to provide its own training as soon as possible. Resources may be necessary to fund parent aides, parent involvement activities, and social skills curriculum materials. The most critical requirement for the model to function is that the staff believe in the underlying philosophy and assumptions concerning shared decision making, the whole-child perspective, and the high expectation for student success. The model is designed to work at the school level rather than the classroom level. The major components of this program follow.

1. *Governance and management team.* The governance and management team is representative of all adults involved in the school, consisting of the principal, two teachers, three parents, and a mental health team member. Leadership of the group is at the discretion of the school, but the principal mainly chairs the team meetings. The team should meet on a weekly basis. All decisions should be made on the consensus of all members of the team. The group's main goal is to (1) establish policy guidelines to address curriculum, social climate, and staff development; (2) carry out systematic school planning, resource assessment and mobilization, program implementation, evaluation and modification of the curriculum, and social climate and staff development areas; (3) coordinate activities of all individuals, groups, and programs in school; and (4) work with the parent group to plan an annual social (activity) calendar.

2. *Mental health team.* The mental health team consists of a classroom teacher, a special education teacher, a social worker, and the school psychologist. The team also works as a governance group, integrating mental health principles with the functioning of all school activities. The team serves individual teachers by suggesting in-classroom ways to manage early and potential problem behaviors. It also trains faculty and personnel to provide a variety of child development and mental health services. The team should act in a preventive mode rather than a crisis response mode.

3. *Curriculum and staff development.* Curriculum and staff development are part of the plan developed by the governance team. This component provides instruction, direction, and support to teachers to enhance the quality of education received by children. The goal is to integrate mental health into curriculum activities. This is where a social skills curriculum is being encouraged.

Although there is a long history of school use of the program, the evaluation evidence is limited. A recent document summarizes published studies on the model (Department of Education Planning and Evaluation Service, 1997).

The Paideia Program

The Paideia program, outlined by Mortmer Adler (1982) in *The Paideia Proposal: An Educational Manifesto,* was designed for learners of all ages in grades K-12 and has been implemented in elementary, middle, and secondary schools. The program promotes the idea that all children are entitled to the same education in terms of content and instructional methodology. There are no set guidelines for implementing the program, however, and schools wishing to implement the program must base implementation on their own understanding of the idea. The program is based on great works of literature, and teaching skills are not usually part of teacher education programs. Few resources outside of the purchase of great books are required. Teacher training is difficult, although it can be accomplished by having a small group of strong teachers who can strengthen the skills of the weaker teachers.

Adler's (1982) Paideia program uses three methods of instruction: didactic, coaching, and Socratic seminar. *Didactic* instruction is the kind of instruction currently found in classrooms where "teacher talk" is the focus of instruction. *Coaching* is described as one-on-one instruction in which the teacher works closely with the student to improve his or her skills. The centerpiece of the Paideia concept is *Socratic seminars,* discussions among students and teachers that explore many ideas. The program is unique because it allows equal opportunity for all learners to discuss ideas, allows teachers to become instructional facilitators who seek knowledge along with the students rather than being a cornucopia of knowledge, and requires teachers to provide individual instruction to help meet each students' needs during the development of skills (Department of Education and Planning Service, 1997).

Outcomes-Based Education

Although there has been controversy regarding outcomes-based education (OBE), it is a recent restructuring initiative that is worthy of school leaders' consideration or adaptation because OBE reflects the belief that for organizations to get where they are going, they must first determine where they are and where they want to be (see, e.g., Covey's, 1990, second habit of highly effective people—"begin with the end in mind"). The objective then is to plan backward to determine the best course to get from a present state (here) to a desired future state (there). Spady and Marshall (1991) refer to this process as *design down* from identified exit outcomes and then *deliver up* through instruction. An important consideration for educators in this premise is that the outcomes approach provides many paths to the desired outcomes for all types of learners to follow, not just a culminating exam based on factual information.

What, then, is a good definition of OBE? Minnesota, one of the first states to adopt OBE, provides a useful definition. OBE is a pupil-centered, results-oriented system based on the belief that all individuals can learn. In this system, (1) what a pupil learns is clearly identified; (2) each pupil's progress is based on his or her demonstrated achievement; (3) each pupil's needs are accommodated through multiple instructional strategies and assessment tools; and (4) each pupil is provided time and assistance to realize her or his potential (Minnesota Department of Education, 1996).

The OBE model, then, determines what skills and knowledge students need to be successful when they leave the system (exit outcomes). Those skills then drive the components of the system, that is, curriculum, instruction, and assessment. The OBE model emphasizes higher-order thinking skills such as analysis, problem solving, and integration of knowledge. Student progress is assessed by a variety of methods, including tests, teacher observations, anecdotal records, checklists, and portfolios. An example of an outcome might be "Students will use language effectively with a variety of audiences to inform, explain, describe, and narrate."

Some 36 states have either adopted or are considering OBE for school improvement. OBE is attracting large numbers of adherents because a deeply committed group of OBE pioneers has fostered major improvements in student learning during the past decade in school districts, individual schools, and a variety of subject areas. These successes have validated the three philosophical premises of OBE: (1) All students can learn and succeed, but not on the same day or in the same way; (2) success breeds success; and (3) schools control the conditions of success.

The teachers believe that all students can learn. Students know what is expected of them. Students may have as many learning experiences as necessary to achieve success. Success breeds success because teachers empower students to reach the outcomes taught knowing that all students must experience success daily. And schools control the conditions of success: curriculum, instruction, assessment, allocation of time, and opportunities for learning. In an OBE system, the teacher makes a difference. The ability and opportunity to intervene in a child's life in a positive way is education at its purest level.

OBE is an optimistic philosophy that focuses on human potential. The power of the OBE framework lurks in the "thinking" and "hearts" of its advocates. It is the generative power of OBE that fosters a commitment to excellence. OBE is based on four key principles: (1) clarity of focus on outcomes of significance, (2) expanded opportunity and support for learning success, (3) high expectations for all to succeed, and (4) design down from ultimate outcomes.

Clarity of focus means making that culminating demonstration the starting point, focal point, and ultimate goal of curriculum design and instruction and carefully aligning (matching) curriculum, instruction, assessment, and credentialing with the substance (i.e., criteria) and processes of the intended demonstration.

Design down means that curriculum and instructional design inherently should carefully proceed backward from the culminating demonstrations (i.e., outcomes) on which everything ultimately focuses and rests, thereby assuring that all the components required for a successful culminating demonstration are in place.

High expectations means that outcomes should represent a high level of challenge for students, and all should be expected to accomplish them eventually at high performance levels and be given credit for that high-level performance whenever it occurs.

Expanded opportunity means that time should be used as a flexible resource rather than as a predefined absolute in both instructional design and delivery (to match differences in student learning rates better, i.e., aptitudes) and also that students should deliberately be allowed at least more than one uniform, routine chance to receive needed instruction and to demonstrate their learning successfully.

According to Spady and Marshall (1991), the four major operational components of OBE are curriculum, instruction, assessment, and advancement. The way these concepts are used in relation to outcomes is the critical component of OBE. Outcomes are action statements that tell what a student will know or do upon completion of the learning experience. They are arranged into five categories—knowledge, inquiry and problem-solving skills, psychomotor skills, social skills, and values. No one category is more important than any other, and all may be found in one curriculum area. The highest-level outcomes are

exit outcomes, and they must be demonstrated for a student to graduate from a K-12 OBE system. There are also outcomes for programs,
units, and lessons and for movement to another academic level. Each
of these outcomes must relate to and support the exit outcomes.

Curriculum.

1. Outcomes determine the curriculum.

2. Activities focus on the learner and the outcome rather than on
   the curriculum.

3. Activities become the experiences or tools of learning.

4. Assessment is criterion referenced (rather than norm referenced), so students are assessed on what they know or can do
   as it relates to the outcome, rather than based on the achievement of other students.

5. The standard of excellence (mastery) on an assessment stays
   consistent for all students and is used as a diagnostic tool.

Instruction.

1. OBE teachers are concerned with teaching concepts and skills,
   not with covering material.

2. The emphasis is always on the learner.

3. In an OBE program, there is close alignment with outcomes,
   instruction, and assessment.

4. Students must be told what it is they are learning and how it
   will be assessed; there should be no mystery lessons or hidden
   agendas.

5. Empowering the student often leads to making the teacher a
   colearner.

6. Teaching time and learning time are not always the same.

7. Assessment should not occur until learning time is over.

Assessment.

1. The purpose of assessment is to document student progress.

2. Daily work or learning experiences should not be used to determine a final grade, but rather as an indication of readiness for the formal assessment that would determine the final grade.

3. Because some students learn at different paces, documentation procedures that show the learner's growth and progress are necessary.

Advancement.

1. Teachers focus on development of the learner and her or his ability to move ahead.

2. Teachers organize their classes to promote learning and require students to demonstrate skills and the acquisition of knowledge before moving them on to other courses, outcomes, or grades.

Electronic Communities

Our world is changing, and technology is changing the way we do business. Carroll (1997) indicates, however, that technology is changing our way of life everywhere except in the schools. He states that we still have Industrial Age schools in an Information Age, with less than 10% of the classrooms fully equipped with computers. The basic technology remains the chalk and chalkboard. Consequently, there are massive numbers of disadvantaged students, teachers, and parents across the country who do not have access to learning resources.

As a response to this need, the U.S. Department of Education sponsors Challenge Grants for Technology in Education, which build electronic communities and are designed to stimulate local innovations in the use of new learning technologies. Since 1995, these efforts have awarded 43 districts $300,000 to $1.9 million per year for 5 years. Challenge Grants build electronic communities and are catalysts for reform. Joining forces to transform schools, they bring together communities of educators, parents, business and industry partners, hardware and software manufacturers, telecommunication firms, universities, and libraries. A myriad of learning communities can be found on the Web that can enhance the learning and awareness of students.

Student competency in challenging subjects is at the core of every school district curriculum. As educational leaders assist students in developing these competencies, they need to be cognizant of creating environments and structures in which students can think critically. Critical thinkers are more responsible citizens. Administrators can construct such environments through programs described in this chapter. Each program includes the collaboration of various school district entities to ensure a future with productive and responsible citizens.

References

Adler, M. J. (1982). *The Paideia proposal: An educational manifesto.* New York: Macmillan.

Atkin, J. M., & Karplus, R. (1962). Discovery or invention? *Science Teacher, 29*(5), 45.

Beilin, H., & Pufall, P. B. (1992). *Piaget's theory: Prospects and possibilities.* Hillsdale, NJ: Laurence Erlbaum.

Boyer, E. L. (1995). *The basic school: A community for learning.* Princeton, NJ: Carnegie Foundation for the Advancement of Teaching.

Bracey, G. W. (1996). The sixth Bracey report on the condition of public education. *Phi Delta Kappan, 78*(2), 127-138.

Brooks, J. G., & Brooks, M. G. (1993). *The case for constructivist classrooms.* Alexandria, VA: Association for Supervision and Curriculum Development.

Carroll, T. G. (1997). Challenge grants: Bringing schools into the information age. *Principal, 76*(3), 26-28.

Center for Critical Thinking. (1997). *Critical thinking and the redesign of instruction.* Santa Rosa, CA: Author.

Comer, J. P. (1980). *School power: Implication of an intervention project.* New York: Free Press.

Covey, S. F. (1990). *The 7 habits of highly effective people.* New York: Simon & Schuster.

Cuban, L. (1988). A fundamental puzzle of school reform. *Phi Delta Kappan, 70,* 341-344.

Cuban, L. (1990). Reforming again, again, and again. *Educational Researcher, 19,* 3-13.

Department of Education, National Center for Education Statistics. (1994). *America's challenge—Accelerating academic achieve-*

ment: NAEP's assessment of fourth, eighth, and twelfth graders. Washington, DC: Government Printing Office.

Department of Education Planning and Evaluation Service. (1997). *Special strategies for educating disadvantaged children. Final report.* Washington, DC: Department of Education.

Foundation for Critical Thinking. (1997). *Critical thinking and the redesign of instruction.* Unpublished manuscript (Available from Foundation for Critical Thinking, Santa Rosa, CA).

Halford, G. S. (1993). *Children's understanding: The development of mental models.* Hillsdale, NJ: Lawrence Erlbaum.

Lieberman, A. (1992). The meaning of scholarly activity and the building of community. *Education Research, 21* (6), 5-12.

Lieberman, A., & Miller, L. (1990). Restructuring schools: What matters and what works. *Phi Delta Kappan, 72,* 29-34.

Madden, N. A., Slavin, R. E., Karweit, N. L., Dolan, L., & Wasik, B. A. (1991). Success for all. *Phi Delta Kappan, 72,* 593-599.

Marzano, R. J. (1992). *A different kind of classroom: Teaching with dimensions of learning.* Alexandria, VA: Association for Supervision and Curriculum Development.

McClelland, S., Marsh, G. E., & Podemski, R. S. (1994). Trends and issues in the 1993 professional education literature. *School Library Media Annual, 12,* 234-243.

McManus, M. M., & Aiken, R. M. (1995). Monitoring computer-based collaborative problem solving. *Journal of Artificial Intelligence in Education, 6* (4), 307-336.

Minnesota Department of Education. (1996). *Outcomes-based education.* St. Paul: Author.

National Committee on Science Education Standards and Assessment. (1996). *National science education standards.* Washington, DC: National Academy Press.

National Council of Teachers of Mathematics. (1989). *Curriculum and evaluation standards for school mathematics.* Reston, VA: Author.

Piaget, J. (1970). Piaget's theory. In P. Mussen (Ed.), *Carmichael's manual of child psychology* (Vol. 1, pp.703-732). New York: John Wiley.

Presseisen, B. Z. (1986). *Thinking skills: Research and practice.* Washington, DC: National Education Association.

Quinlan, L. A. (1997). Creating a classroom kaleidoscope. *Educational Technology, 37* (3), 15-22.

Resnick, L. B., & Klopfer, L. E. (1989). *Toward the thinking curriculum: Current cognitive research.* Alexandria, VA: Association for Supervision and Curriculum Development.

Schunk, D. H., & Zimmerman, B. J. (1994). *Self-regulation of learning and performance.* Hillsdale, NJ: Lawrence Erlbaum.

Sizer, T. R. (1984). *Horace's compromise: The dilemma of the American high school.* Boston: Houghton Mifflin.

Sizer, T. R. (1992). *Horace's school: Redesigning the American high school.* Boston: Houghton Mifflin.

Sizer, T. R. (1997). *Horace's hope.* Boston: Houghton Mifflin.

Slavin, R. (1990). *Cooperative learning: Theory, research, and practice.* Englewood Cliffs, NJ: Prentice Hall.

Spady, W. G., & Marshall, K. J. (1991). Beyond traditional outcome-based education. *Educational Leadership, 49,* 67-72.

Starr, R. (1997). Delivering instruction on the World Wide Web: Overview and basic design principles. *Educational Technology, 37*(3), 7-14.

Steffe, L. P., & Gale, J. (1995). *Constructivism in education.* Hillsdale, NJ: Lawrence Erlbaum.

Strommen, E. F., & Lincoln, B. (1992). Constructivism, technology, and the future of classroom learning. *Education and Urban Society, 24,* 466-476.

Timar, T. (1989). The politics of school restructuring. *Phi Delta Kappan, 71,* 265-275.

CHAPTER 4

Every Teacher Prepared

By the year 2000, the nation's teaching force will have access to programs for the continued improvement of their professional skills and the opportunity to acquire the knowledge and skills needed to instruct and prepare all American students for the next century.
(Goals 2000: Educate America Act of 1994)

The current education reform movement was triggered by the report of the National Commission on Excellence in Education (1983), *A Nation at Risk*. Three subsequent reports shifted the national spotlight to the teacher education arena, those of the Holmes Group (1986), the Carnegie Task Force on Teaching as a Profession (1986), and the Renaissance Group (1989). All merit the serious attention of schools of education, state departments of education, and involved leaders from public and private school systems. Nevertheless, the Holmes Group has had the most enduring influence on the revolution in the teaching profession.

Research: Revolution in the Teaching Profession

There are three paths toward revolutionizing the teaching profession: restructuring teacher training, changing the conditions under which teachers work, and providing continuous professional development.

Box 4.1. What the Research Says About . . .

Restructuring Teacher Training

◆ All teacher candidates should have a broadly based, liberal
   arts undergraduate education, with at least one subject major
   (Carnegie Task Force on Teaching as a Profession, 1986;
   Chase, 1998; Feldman, 1998; Holmes Group, 1986, 1990,
   1995).

◆ All prospective teachers should have a well-structured induction program that includes a 1-year internship under the
   supervision of an experienced knowledgeable teacher (Wise,
   Darling-Hammond, & Gendler, 1990).

◆ A new national nongovernmental board of the teaching profession composed of the majority of experienced teachers
   should be created; the board should develop professional
   standards for teaching on the basis of the knowledge and the
   clinical practice base in teaching and oversee the development
   of a new national assessment procedure for the professional
   certification of prospective teachers (Buday & Kelly, 1996;
   Carnegie Task Force, 1986; Shanker, 1996).

◆ Board certification for new teachers should be awarded only
   upon successful completion of a rigorous teacher education
   program, passage of a national teacher entrance examination
   developed by the profession, and demonstrated teaching competence in intern and residency programs (Buday & Kelly,
   1996; Carnegie Task Force, 1986; Shanker, 1996; Wise et al.,
   1990).

Changing the Conditions
Under Which Teachers Work

◆ In the future, experienced teachers should be eligible for professional career advancement through advanced certification
   by the new national professional board (Buday & Kelly, 1996;
   Carnegie Task Force, 1986; Shanker, 1996).

◆ Teachers should have a variety of opportunities for performing professional roles and advancing within the teaching profession, while continuing to be practicing teachers (Carnegie Task Force, 1986; Chase, 1998; Darling-Hammond, 1997; Feldman, 1998; National Commission on Teaching and America's Future, 1996; Seashore-Louis & Kruse, 1995).

◆ Teaching must be structured as a lifetime career. Teaching and educational administration must be considered as two separate careers, and teacher salaries should not be limited to those paid to school administrators (Carnegie Task Force, 1986; Chase, 1998; Feldman, 1998).

◆ All decisions regarding the establishment, maintenance, or reform of school structure and governance must be based on their effect on student learning (Carnegie Task Force, 1986; Cawelti, 1995; Darling- Hammond, 1996; Elmore, 1996; National Foundation, 1996).

◆ A great deal has been written and discussed concerning effective schools; such schools are learning centered. Descriptions of academically effective, learning-centered schools share common characteristics such as clear goals related to academic learning, high expectations for students and faculty, strong leadership in support of the learning goals of the school, collegial relationships and collaborative planning among teachers and administrators, learning time given priority, frequent student assessment and feedback, a safe and orderly climate with clear and fairly enforced discipline codes, and schoolwide continuous professional development (Goodlad, 1998; Joyce & Showers, 1988; Office of Education Research and Improvement, 1993).

◆ School faculty and staff must share in the establishment and maintenance of school goals and values consistent with required local, state, and national education outcomes (Sparks & Hirsh, 1997).

(continued)

Box 4.1. Continued

◆ School site autonomy must be increased, with greater decision-making power invested in classroom teachers (Sparks & Hirsh, 1997).

◆ Teachers should be the instructional leaders of the schools and should be responsible for making decisions about instructional strategies, professional development, curricular materials, pupil assignments and scheduling, structure of learning time during the school day, instructional goals beyond those set by the state or local school board, school-level budgetary matters, and elements of professional evaluation (Guskey & Huberman, 1995; National Foundation, 1996).

Providing Continuous
Professional Development

◆ Some researchers suggest that professional development efforts should be teacher specific and focus on day-to-day activities at the classroom level (Rigden, 1996); others indicate that an emphasis on individuals is detrimental to progress and more systemic or organizational approaches are necessary (National Staff Development Council, 1994).

Applying Research to Practice:
Developing an Action Plan

A major goal of the teacher education reform movement is to redesign teacher education programs with the objective of initiating a significant reconceptualization of how and where teachers are prepared. To accomplish the program redesign goals, the Holmes Group (1986, 1990, 1995), the Carnegie Task Force (1986), and the Renaissance Group (1989) call for making the teaching profession, and teacher education, more rigorous and prestigious. To improve the prestige of teachers, the Holmes Group suggests that colleges of education become "professional" schools like colleges of law and medicine

◆ Some scholars stress that reforms in professional development must be initiated and carried out by individual teachers and school-based personnel (Fullan & Hargreaves, 1996); others emphasize that the most successful programs are guided by a clear vision that transcends the walls of individual classrooms and schools, because individual teachers and school-based individuals generally lack the opportunity to conceive and implement worthwhile improvements (Barth, 1991; Stallings, 1991).

◆ Some experts argue that the most effective professional development programs approach change in a gradual and incremental fashion, not expecting too much at one time (Stallings & Kowalski, 1990); others insist that the broader the scope of a professional development program, the more effort required of teachers, and the greater the overall change in teaching style attempted, the more likely the program is to elicit the enthusiasm of teachers and to be implemented well (McIntire, 1995; Reynolds, 1996; Teitel, 1996).

and that teachers be prepared through graduate-level programs, rather than in undergraduate degree programs in education. In restructuring efforts, leaders in schools should consider the following strategies and should determine what is reasonable for them to accomplish in schools and institutions of higher education.

Strategy 1: Consider Holmes Group Standards

The Holmes Group is a national organization of 100 research universities dedicated to solving problems associated with the generally low quality of teacher preparation in the United States. The initial focus of the Holmes Group was on improving teacher education programs and sharing a kindred institutional orientation toward research.

The Holmes Group challenges the 250 leading research universities to engage in a serious commitment to quality, first in their own institutions and then in others throughout the nation. The universities in which these 250 education schools reside have a tremendous effect on the remaining 1,000 places that educate teachers and other educators. These research universities develop the knowledge base for the field of education; they influence education policy; and they prepare most of the individuals who attain leadership positions in the education establishment.

The Holmes Group recently released its latest publication, *Tomorrow's Schools of Education* (1995). This report was preceded by two other major publications: *Tomorrow's Teachers* (1986), which outlines a new plan for preparing teachers, and *Tomorrow's Schools* (1990), which describes the principles for design of professional development schools.

The Holmes Group (1995) challenges the 250 leading research universities to raise their standards of quality by doing the following:

Redesigning the Curriculum

Here studies focus on the learning needs of the young and the development of educators across their careers—replacing studies less focused on youngsters' learning and development, organized by segregated roles for educators, and centered on initial credentialing.

Developing a New Faculty

Now a clear minority, the numbers of university faculty who are as at home working in the public schools as on the university campus will come to make up the majority of the education school faculty. Board-certified teachers and other qualified practitioners will join these faculty as colleagues in conducting important research and in better educating the nation's educators.

Recruiting a Culturally Diverse Student Body

Before the next generation of educators retires, almost half of the nation's youngsters (46%) will be from one or another minority group. The nation's education workforce—teachers, administrators, counselors, and those who educate educators—must be more diverse than today. Programs must be mounted to recruit, retain, and graduate highly diverse groups of education leaders at initial and advanced levels.

Creating Professional Development Schools

Instead of working predominantly on campus and occasionally in schools across the American landscape, faculty and students will do much of their work in *professional development schools* (PDS). These are real public schools selected and joined in partnership with the university for their innovative spirit and serious intent to improve the quality of learning for educators and students.

Building Networks at Local, State, and National Levels

Long too remote from the professionals and public they serve, the education schools will together form an interconnecting set of networks at local, state, regional, and national levels to ensure better work and accountability (Holmes Group, 1995).

Strategy 2: Create Professional Development Schools

The Holmes Group emphasizes the academic and field experience components of professional education and their close articulation. The Holmes Group recommends establishing PDSs within public school districts analogous to teaching hospitals in medicine. The PDSs are unique in their ability to combine research, teacher training, and development of new models of teaching and learning simultaneously. Although initiatives have addressed these concerns separately in the past, the PDSs will permit the orchestration of a future vision of what schools will be like.

A PDS is a commitment by a school of education and public schools to ensure student success and achievement. A PDS is a preparation site for preservice educators and for the continuing professional development of educators.

A PDS offers far more than just a clinical setting. It is a comprehensive collaboration for school innovation, where a substantial amount of inquiry is ongoing. University faculty and PDS teachers are able to develop common research questions that link practical knowledge with scholarly pursuits. The PDS provides a place for university faculty to help shape quality programs that serve as models of learning, inquiry, reflection, technology, innovation, and professionalism.

The PDS provides a place for the new kind of professional who is equally at home in the university and in the school, and who works in both settings. The PDS provides an indispensable context for this professional, as an institution where school and university personnel regularly meet in joint and collaborative work. PDS teachers serve as clinical instructors for professional preparation programs, and each master teacher holds an adjunct faculty status with the school of education (Darling-Hammond, 1994).

According to a survey of the American Association of Colleges for Teacher Education (AACTE; 1996), there are currently more than 400 PDSs nationwide. Many of these teaching laboratories are associated with institutions accredited by the National Council for the Accreditation of Teacher Education (NCATE). As a result, NCATE is in the process of developing standards for PDSs that can be applied in lieu of the NCATE traditional approaches to teacher education standards used during on-site accreditation visits.

Common ground can be found in the statements of purposes and principles made by networks and groups that have pioneered the PDS concept. These include the Holmes Group, the National Network for Educational Renewal, the National Center for Restructuring Education, School, and Teaching (NCREST), the National Education Association Teacher Education Initiative, the AFT Professional Practices Project, and various state partnerships and networks.

These groups commonly agree that PDSs represent partnerships between schools and universities that come together for the following purposes:

1. To support the simultaneous renewal of schools and colleges of education

2. To provide clinical education for new teachers in restructuring settings

3. To support continuing professional development

4. To support inquiry directed at the improvement of practice

The following criteria have emerged already for identifying PDS sites:

■ University and K-12 school faculty share a learner-centered approach to teaching and learning.

■ There is parity between school and university within the collaboration.

■ Issues of equity are addressed in the partnership.

Strategy 3: Develop Teaching Internships

To replace the "sink or swim" approach to teacher training, Arthur Wise, Linda Darling-Hammond, and Tamar Gendler (1990) propose that a paid internship be required for aspiring teachers. Under the current system, the typical message to a new teacher is: figure it out for yourself; do it all yourself; and keep it to yourself.

Instead of that makeshift system, the RAND Center for the Study of the Teaching Profession recommends a 1-year formal training program similar to those for engineers, architects, and physicians. The program would emphasize hands-on training along with guidance, support, and, as the year progresses, increased responsibility. Teaching children means being prepared for complexity. Due to that complexity, even well-intentioned initiatives such as student-teacher programs and mentoring may fall short.

Under the plan, students would serve as teaching interns after they graduate from college but before they could apply for a license. The primary purpose: to weed out the unqualified and provide a support system for the best teacher candidates. The interns would observe senior teachers and teach some classes, gradually progressing to greater degrees of responsibility. Interns also would teach students of different ages in urban, rural, and suburban settings.

Senior teachers and a director would head the internship programs. School districts could recruit current teachers for short or long stints to guide interns, consult with them, observe them, evaluate them, and share the responsibility for teaching their students. In addition, certain schools would be designated as "teaching laboratories" or PDSs. Most of those would be schools with state-of-the-art teaching to typically underserved populations.

Although interns should be paid, the delicate issue of salary should be left up to individual states and localities. Because many interns will have only a part-time teaching load, school districts do not necessarily have to offer full-time pay, yet failing to offer any pay could discourage students from taking part. Union membership could be a potential stumbling block. To diffuse that issue, creating a partial union membership for interns may solve the problem.

A set of guidelines for a teacher internship program has been developed in Minnesota. The state is reviewing the guidelines and plans to ask the state legislature to fund a pilot program. If funded, every pilot program in the state would involve more than one school district and have a director who would select faculty and staff (Wise, Darling-Hammond, & Gendler, 1990).

Strategy 4: Consider the Renaissance Group Principles

The Renaissance Group is a distinguished national group of 21 state colleges and universities that have as their focus a major commitment to teacher education. In 1989, the Renaissance Group reached consensus in its landmark publication, *Teachers for the New World,* a statement of the principles of quality programs for the preparation of teachers. This group emphasizes that teachers for the future must

- have an in-depth knowledge of subject matter
- be skilled at constructing and using metaphors appropriate to understanding the subject matter
- understand the structure of knowledge of the disciplines they will be teaching and the interrelationship of knowledge from various disciplines
- understand sequencing learning experiences and be able to match their teaching with the experiences and cultural backgrounds of their students
- be articulate about their plans and designs for instruction and dedicated to their careers in teaching
- understand education as a social system and how school links to other community agencies
- use their knowledge and skills to assist our children and youth to have a sense of fulfillment and an appreciation of life's experiences and to become productive workers and capable leaders in the new world

Another new element, according to the Renaissance Group, for new world schools is the preparation of effective educational administrators. School administrators must be skilled in ways of leading educational personnel in teaching and learning. They must be visionary and at the same time skilled in knowing how to manage and structure complicated social systems. This requires an understanding of how to initiate and manage change to facilitate school improvements and innovation. School administrators must also understand and appreciate the role of teachers in providing leadership in the new world of schools.

In addition to these viewpoints regarding teachers and administrators, the Renaissance Group identifies a set of principles that are both statements of best practice for the preparation of teachers and objectives to be achieved within colleges and universities that strive for a quality program for the preparation of teachers.

Principle 1. The education of teachers is an all-campus responsibility.

Principle 2. Programs for the preparation of teachers thrive in a university culture that values quality teaching.

Principle 3. Decisions concerning the education of teachers are the shared responsibility of the university faculty, practitioners, and other related professionals.

Principle 4. The initial preparation of teachers is integrated throughout a student's university experience and is not segmented or reserved to the student's final year.

Principle 5. The appropriate role of the state is to establish outcome expectations for teacher education graduates; the appropriate role of the university is to determine the curriculum, standards, and internal policies for teacher education programs.

Principle 6. Rigorous learning expectations and exit requirements characterize the program to educate teachers.

Principle 7. The academic preparation of teachers includes a rigorous general education program, in-depth subject matter preparation, and both general and content-specific preparation in teaching methodology.

Principle 8. Teacher education programs reflect American diversity and prepare graduates to teach in a pluralistic and multicultural society.

Principle 9. The education of teachers incorporates extensive and sequenced field and clinical experiences.

Principle 10. Quality teacher preparation programs have faculty who are active in scholarly and professional endeavors.

Principle 11. The continuing professional development of teachers and other education personnel is the shared responsibility of the university faculty and other education professionals.

Principle 12. Programs to educate teachers for the new world have sufficient support to implement these principles. This support may take many forms, including a reaffirmation by the education community of the importance of teacher education and additional finances to keep abreast of challenging new social and technological changes (Renaissance Group, 1989).

Strategy 5: Reform Educational Administration Programs

Every educational reform report since the 1980s has concluded that schools are only as good as their administrators. The prospect of inadequately trained school leaders is serious when one considers the public schools' struggle with such problems as declining test scores, drug abuse, school violence and vandalism, at-risk youngsters, and AIDS. It is not surprising therefore that calls for reform of university programs for the preparation of school administrators have resounded throughout the nation.

Criticism of administrator preparation programs has been ongoing for some time. In 1987, the National Commission on Excellence in Educational Administration made eight specific recommendations for the improvement of university programs for the preparation of school administrators, including the establishment of a national policy board for educational administration, the abolishment of educational administration programs at 300 institutions offering such programs, and the reformation of state licensure programs for school administrators.

The latest criticism came in a report released by the National Policy Board for Educational Administration, a coalition of 10 national educational organizations, including the National Association of Elementary School Principals, the National Association of Secondary School Principals, and the National Council of Professors of Educational Administration. The National Policy Board asserted its commitment to the improvement of the preparation of school administrators who will lead our nation's elementary and secondary schools in the future.

The National Policy Board recommends a nine-item agenda for reform in the preparation of school administrators:

1. Mount vigorous recruitment strategies to attract the brightest and most capable candidates of diverse race, ethnicity, and gender, including a minority enrollment at least comparable to the region's minority public school enrollment.

2. Dramatically raise entrance standards to administrator preparation programs to ensure that all candidates possess strong analytic ability (assessed by a standardized national test, with admission to preparation programs limited to individuals scoring in the top quartile), high administrative potential, and demonstrated success in teaching, including a master's degree.

3. Ensure the quality of faculty in administrator preparation programs by strengthening faculty recruitment, selection, and staff development; maintaining at least five full-time faculty members who do the bulk of teaching, advising, and mentoring; and ensuring a student-faculty ratio comparable to other graduate programs.

4. Make the doctorate in educational administration (EdD) a prerequisite to national certification and state licensure for full-time administrators who are in charge of a school or school system and abolish specialist and master's degree programs in educational administration altogether.

5. Include one full-time year of academic residency and one full-time year of field residency in the EdD program. Permit modifications in the type or duration of the clinical residency for candidates with full-time administrative experience in education.

6. Develop the elements of the curriculum to transmit a common core of knowledge and skills, grounded in the problems of practice, including societal and cultural influences, teaching and learning processes, organizational theory, methodologies of organizational studies, leadership and management processes, policy studies, and moral and ethical dimensions of schooling.

7. Establish long-term, formal relationships between universities and school districts to create partnership sites for clinical study, field residency, and applied research.

8. Establish a national professional standards board to develop and administer a national certification examination and encourage states to require candidates for licensure to pass this examination.

9. Withhold national accreditation of administrator preparation programs unless programs meet the standards specified in the National Policy Board's report and require that criteria for state accreditation and program approval include these standards (National Policy Board, 1989).

The reform proposals of the National Policy Board include some controversial ideas, such as the recommendations that prospective school administrators be required to complete 2 years of full-time study (including 1 full-time year of fieldwork), obtain a doctorate degree before being permitted to administer a school or school district, and pass a national certification examination. These three recommendations, in particular, may need to be modified somewhat to be more acceptable to university officials, legislators, state school officers, and practitioners.

The National Policy Board (1993) released a comprehensive program for the preparation of school principals, which marked the culmination of 3 years of research on the knowledge and skills required to lead schools into the 21st century. More than 100 principals, professors of education, and private-sector training officials were involved in the effort, which was financed by grants from the Danforth and Geraldine R. Dodge Foundation and the Lilly Endowment.

The 570-page document (National Policy Board, 1993) was designed as a new structure by which to organize the principalship and takes as its departure point 21 performance "domains." The domains are the key behaviors, skills, and areas of knowledge that provide the foundation for the principalship.

The National Policy Board, together with the American Association of School Administrators (AASA), developed standards for the American superintendency (American Association of School Administrators, 1993). The draft standards encompass 11 domains in four broad areas of leadership: strategic, organizational, instructional, and political and community. The draft guidelines include a requirement that institutions have a 6-month structured internship experience as part of their superintendent preparation programs. Other areas receiving increased attention are leadership, skill development, planning and evaluating instructional programs, and ethics.

Several efforts are underway across the United States to restructure preparation programs for school administrators (see Box 4.2). Universities, school districts, and state boards of education are at work revamping curricula; forging stronger relationships between universities and local school systems; and insisting on practical exercises, fieldwork, and internships for prospective administrators (Stover, 1990).

Strategy 6: Emphasize Professional Growth and Development

Every proposal to reform and restructure schools emphasizes professional development as an important vehicle in efforts to bring about the necessary change. This section provides a series of guidelines for professional development, drawn primarily from research on professional development specifically and on the change process generally (Astuto, Clark, Read, McGree, & Pelton Fernandez, 1994; Cawelti, 1994; Fine, 1994; Finn & Walberg, 1994; Fuhrman & O'Day, 1996; Fullan, 1991, 1993; Glickman, 1993; Goldring & Rallis, 1993; Harvey, 1995; Herman & Herman, 1994; Hess, 1995; Lieberman, 1995; Lieberman & Miller, 1991; Lotto & Thurston, 1990; Maeroff, 1993; McDonald, 1996; Murphy, 1991; O'Hanlon, 1996; Sarason, 1995, 1996; Schmuck & Runkel, 1994).

Due to the dynamic influence of contextual environments, it is impossible to make precise statements about the components of an effective professional development program that will work in all situations. Nevertheless, Guskey and Huberman (1995) provide the

(text continues on p. 82)

Box 4.2. Vignettes: Restructuring Efforts Underway

Stanford University: Problem-Based Program

The School of Education at Stanford University recently began a new principal preparation program rooted in three basic assumptions about the instructional process: (1) instruction should be problem based; (2) it should emphasize the view that leadership entails getting results through others; and (3) it should encourage self-directed learning (Bridges, 1992).

Stanford's program is composed of three distinct instructional components, including regular courses, problem-based practicums, and an internship. The coursework makes up 60% of the students' university-based program of study. Students spend the remaining 40% of their time at the university in a practicum.

The practicums are organized into instructional blocks made up of problems frequently encountered by elementary, middle, and high school principals. Students work in small groups, during flexible time blocks of instruction, to solve a particular problem. Some are assigned to group process roles of project leader, facilitator, or recorder. The role of each student varies from block to block. The small groups are provided a wide range of physical and human resources, including participating professors as well as practicing principals from the area. Summer classes provide an opportunity for full-time study in cohort groups of 12 to 18 students.

University of Colorado at Denver:
Problem-Based Program

The School of Education at the University of Colorado at Denver (UCD) also has developed a problem-based program for the preparation of principals. The program was developed collaboratively with school administrators through a partnership of UCD faculty in the divisions of administration, curriculum, and supervision; local school district principals; and private sector executives from IBM, Hewlett Packard, U.S. West, and Storage Tek.

UCD's program is innovative in that university faculty from several divisions, practicing school principals, and private sector executives coteach and supervise problem-solving experiences in several modules. Traditional coursework is limited, and much of the learning occurs in "problem blocks" in which faculty/administrator/executive coaches assist students in developing solutions to difficult administrative practice problems.

Stanford's and UCD's problem-based programs were inspired by recent developments in medical education in Europe and the United States. At Harvard University, for example, medical students no longer begin their training with 2 years of theoretical studies. Instead, they are formed into small teams and, under the supervision of regular and clinical faculty, tackle medical problems from the beginning. Research indicates that students in problem-based medical programs such as this learn better and can access knowledge more readily (National Policy Board, 1990).

National Alliance for Developing School Leaders

The National Alliance for Developing School Leaders came into existence in 1990. This project represents a response to the call for change in preparation programs for school administrators. The alliance consists of four universities: Brigham Young University, East Tennessee University, Florida State University, and Virginia Polytechnic Institute, and the National Association of Secondary School Principals (NASSP). The primary funding source for the project is the Danforth Foundation.

Three major objectives provide the framework for the alliance initiative: (1) to change the way principal preparation occurs; (2) to determine the applicability of NASSP administrator-training materials in restructured program models; and (3) to share the findings and results of the project with other universities as a means of modifying principal preparation programs throughout the country (National Association of Secondary School Principals, 1994).

(continued)

Box 4.2. Continued

Duquesne University: Interdisciplinary Program

In the summer of 1994, Duquesne's Interdisciplinary Doctoral Program for Educational Leaders enrolled its first cohort of 36 (American Association of School Administrators, 1994). The cohort is divided into smaller groups of approximately six members each, plus an adviser. Advisers visit cohort members in their work settings twice a year. In addition, each member of the cohort selects a mentor who works with the participant for a 3-year period, judging the student's success or failure in meeting practicum requirements. In developing its practicum, Duquesne's program relies heavily on the advice of local education leaders and AASA's Standards for the American Superintendency.

Duquesne faculty as well as mentors are trained to use electronic networks to facilitate regular communication. Cross-disciplinary study (in psychology, sociology, social psychology, economics, and education) includes instruction via practitioner seminars, simulations, case studies, and field studies. Course content focuses on leadership and district culture, policy and governance, communications and community relations, organizational management, curriculum planning and development, instructional management, human resources management, and values and ethics of leadership. In learning content, heavy emphasis is placed on team building, shared leadership, collaboration, and instructional improvement.

Sam Houston State University:
Integrated Leadership Program

With the support of the Texas Higher Education Coordinating Board and the Texas State University System Board of Regents, the Department of Educational Leadership and Counseling in the College of Education and Applied Science at Sam Houston State University developed the Center for Research and Doctoral Studies in Educational Leadership (CRDSEL). The purpose of CRDSEL is to serve as a support structure that integrates scholarship, teaching, research, mentoring, and field service in educational leadership.

Faculty, students, and area school leaders work collaboratively to create linkages among faculty research, dissertation research, and reflective practice through the design of collaborative research projects and the dissemination of the results. The Center will advance the reflective practitioner model of the doctoral program. The goals of CRDSEL are to support a climate of inquiry and research for the students, faculty, and mentors participating in the doctoral program; seek financial and collaborative support from governmental agencies, businesses, and professional organizations for the Center's activities; build mentoring resources of school leaders (local, state, national, and international) to support the students enrolled in the doctoral program; provide support for faculty within the university who are not teaching in the doctoral program; build research and support resources in specific areas; and establish and maintain communication networks through databases, technological support services, newsletters, workshops, professional associations, and job-alike networks.

CRDSEL provides a support structure for the newly created doctoral program in educational leadership at Sam Houston State University. The integrated doctoral program requires a concentration in educational leadership consisting of four components: at least 18 hours in a leadership core, 15 hours in a research component, 21 hours in a specialization area (instructional leadership and/or content fields), and 12 hours in cognate electives (selected from graduate courses in business, criminal justice, humanities, library science, professional education, mathematics, sciences, and related areas). The completion of a dissertation and a 1-year supervised internship are also required.

The doctoral program in educational leadership is designed for a cohort group. This means that each year 12 to 15 students are admitted to a specific cohort group and are required to take the four curricular program components at the same time. These are spaced over a 3-year period during three trimesters: summer, fall, and spring.

following procedural guidelines that are critical to the professional development process.

Recognize That Change Is Both an Individual and an Organizational Process

Schools cannot be improved without improving the skills and abilities of the teachers and principals who work in them. Teachers are the ones who ultimately will implement change. Therefore, professional development processes must address their needs and concerns.

To view change as merely an individual process can limit the effectiveness of professional development. Organizational characteristics and system politics cannot be neglected. A negative environment can inhibit any change effort, no matter have much we exhort individuals to persist.

To focus on change as merely an organizational process is equally ineffective, however. A typical device of educational policymakers and school administrators is to tinker with the organizational structure. This communicates to the public symbolically that policymakers are concerned with the performance of the system. Yet evidence shows that such structural change does not lead to changes in how teachers teach, what they teach, or how students learn (Elmore, 1992). To facilitate change, we must look beyond policy and consider the embedded infrastructure that most directly affects the actions of individuals who ultimately implement change—principals and teachers (Lunenburg, 1995; Lunenburg & Ornstein, 1996).

Think Big But Start Small

The most successful professional development programs approach change in an incremental fashion (Lunenburg & Ornstein, 1996). Efforts should be made to illustrate how the new practices can be implemented in ways that are not too disruptive or require a great deal of extra work.

Although the changes advocated in a professional development program must not be overwhelming, they need to be sufficiently broad in scope to challenge professionals. Narrowly conceived projects seldom bring about significant improvement. This is what Guskey and Huberman (1995) mean by "think big."

Professional development efforts should be designed with long-term goals based on a broad vision of what is possible. For example, a program might seek to have all students reading at grade level by the year 2000. At the same time, that vision should be accompanied by a strategic plan that includes specific incremental goals for 1, 2 or 3 years into the future: 50% of students will be reading at grade level in year 1; 70% of students will be reading at grade level in year 2; 90% of students will be reading at grade level by year 3 (Lunenburg, 1994).

Work in Teams

Some measure of discomfort typically accompanies most change efforts. This discomfort will be greatly compounded if participants feel isolated and detached in their implementation efforts. Therefore, it is important that professional development programs involve teams of individuals working together.

To ensure that the teams function effectively and engender broad-based support for professional development efforts, it is important that they involve individuals from all levels of the organization: teachers, noninstructional staff, building and central office administrators, and in some contexts parents and community members.

The teams must be linked to established norms of continuous improvement. That is, teamwork must have the expectation that all involved in the change process are constantly seeking and assessing potentially better practices. Such an expectation provides a purpose for meaningful collaboration. In addition, working in teams allows tasks and responsibilities to be shared, reduces the workload of individual team members, and enhances the quality of the work produced.

Provide Feedback on Results

If new practices resulting from professional development programs are to be sustained, participants need to receive feedback on the effects of their efforts. Practices will be accepted and retained when they are perceived as increasing one's competence and effectiveness. This is especially true of teachers, whose primary rewards come from feeling that their practices affect student growth and development. New practices are likely to be abandoned in the absence of positive effects, however. Therefore, specific procedures for feedback on results are essential to the success of professional development efforts.

In most professional development programs involving student learning, teachers receive feedback from their students through regular formative assessments. These can take many forms, including writing samples, skill demonstrations, projects, reports, performance tasks, norm-referenced tests, criterion-referenced tests, and teacher-made tests or quizzes. These periodic checks on student learning provide teachers with evidence of the results of their teaching efforts. These data can then be used to guide revisions in instruction.

Provide Support

Effective implementation of change requires support from top-level administrators such as the superintendent of schools and his or her cabinet. Support from the superintendent usually means that administrators lower in the organization's hierarchy, such as building principals, will be committed to the change. It is particularly important for building principals to manifest supportive and considerate leadership behaviors when change is being implemented. This type of leader behavior includes listening to subordinates' ideas, being approachable, and using employee ideas that have merit. Supportive leaders go out of their way to make the work environment more pleasant and enjoyable. For example, difficult changes may require training to acquire new skills necessary to implement the change. Administrators need to provide such training (Schmuck & Runkel, 1994). In short, when procedures are established to implement changes smoothly, less resistance is likely to be encountered.

When change is imminent, most people say, "What's in it for me?" Subordinates are less likely to resist changes that will benefit them directly (Lawler, 1992). For example, during collective bargaining between the board of education and the teachers' union, certain concessions can be given to teachers in exchange for support of a new program desired by management. Such concessions may include salary increases, bonuses, or more union representation in decision making. Administrators can also use standard rewards such as recognition, increased responsibility, praise, and status symbols. Thus, building in rewards may help reduce subordinates' resistance to change.

Integrate Programs

Education is notorious for introducing a steady stream of changes. Each year new programs are introduced in schools without any effort to show how they relate to the ones that preceded them or those that may come later. Moreover, there is seldom any effort to demonstrate how these various changes contribute to the professional knowledge base.

This pattern of continuous, unrelated change obscures improvement. If professional development efforts that focus on the implementation of changes are to succeed, they must include precise descriptions of how these changes can be integrated. In other words, each new change must be presented as part of a coherent framework for improvement. When several strategies are systematically integrated, substantial improvements become possible.

In recent years, several frameworks for integrating a collection of programs or changes have been developed that teachers are finding useful. For example, Marzano (1992) developed a framework based on various dimensions of learning. Another, developed by Guskey and Huberman (1990), is built around five major components in the teaching and learning process. These frameworks permit skilled teachers to visualize the linkages between various innovations.

Professional Development and Technology

Many schools have determined that one-time inservice training for the entire faculty is ineffective for teachers, particularly for teaching computer use and helping teachers develop methods to use computers as instructional tools (Office of Technology Assessment, 1995). Innovative and relevant professional development programs are needed to meet teachers' diverse needs in technology. Such programs should offer teachers opportunities to learn, practice, and integrate what they learn. In addition, they need to have informal and formal coaching on the new information, techniques, and pedagogy. Mergendoller et al. (1994) suggest that technology should be seen as a means to an end, rather than as an end unto itself.

Mergendoller (1997) reports that "even with a carefully designed professional development program, teachers who succeed in integrating educational technology into their instruction generally do so by spending a great deal of their own time before and after school" (p. 14). According to a study conducted by Mergendoller, Sacks, and Horan (1995), teachers spend an average of 36 hours a year learning how to use technology in their teaching; 60% of that time is spent working by themselves, and 17% of the time is spent in consultation with their colleagues. An even lesser percentage of time, 13%, is spent in inservice sessions or technology courses. Prior to the Mergendoller et al. (1995) study, Marshall (1993) found that many teachers reported that their technology training was too hurried and lacked adequate follow-up support. They also reported that the training usually occurred just before the actual use was to begin; therefore, they complained that assimilation and practice of the newly acquired techniques were not long enough. Regardless of the amount of professional development opportunities afforded to teachers, the major factor, according to Becker (1994), in differentiating schools with exemplary computer-using, technology-integrating teachers is ongoing staff support.

Professional development is critical for the preparation and continued growth of teachers and administrators. Darling-Hammond and McLaughlin (1995) suggest that professional development should provide opportunities for teachers to reflect critically on their practice and to fashion new knowledge and beliefs about content, pedagogy, and learners. Furthermore, they suggest that professional development should prepare teachers to see a complex subject matter from the perspective of diverse students. As Darling-Hammond and McLaughlin (1995) call for a change in the professional development of teachers, Brown and Irby (1997) follow with a call for a change in the professional growth of principals that would enable them to refine leadership practices and increase school effectiveness. Brown and Irby suggest that principals who engage in self-assessment, in problem-solving dialogue with colleagues, in reading to gain information, and in establishing professional goals are principals who direct and enhance not only their own professional development but also the professional development of their faculty.

References

American Association of Colleges for Teacher Education. (1996). *Professional development schools.* Washington, DC: Author.

American Association of School Administrators. (1993). *Professional standards for the superintendency.* Arlington, VA: Author.

American Association of School Administrators. (1994). *Leadership News, 139,* 3.

Astuto, T. A., Clark, D. L., Read, A., McGree, K., & Pelton Fernandez, L. (1994). *Roots of reform: Challenging the assumptions that control in education.* Bloomington, IN: Phi Delta Kappa.

Barth, R. (1991). *Improving schools from within.* San Francisco: Jossey-Bass.

Becker, H. J. (1994). How exemplary computer-using teachers differ from other teachers: Implications for realizing the potential of computer in schools. *Journal of Research on Computing in Education, 26*(3), 291-321.

Bridges, E. M. (1992). *Problem based learning for administrators.* Eugene, OR: ERIC Clearinghouse on Educational Management.

Brown, G., & Irby, B. J. (1997). *The principal portfolio.* Thousand Oaks, CA: Corwin Press.

Buday, M. C., & Kelly, J. A. (1996). National board certification and the teaching profession's commitment to quality assurance. *Phi Delta Kappan, 78*(3), 216.

Carnegie Task Force on Teaching as a Profession. (1986). *A nation prepared: Teachers for the 21st century.* Hyattsville, MD: Author.

Cawelti, G. (1995). *High school restructuring: A national study.* Arlington, VA: Educational Research Service.

Chase, B. (1998). NEA's role in cultivating teachers' professionalism. *Educational Leadership, 55*(5), 18, 20.

Darling-Hammond, L. (1994). *Professional development schools.* New York: Teachers College Press.

Darling-Hammond, L. (1996). Restructuring schools for high performance. In S. Feldman & J. O'Day (Eds.), *Rewards and reform: Creating educational incentives that work.* San Francisco: Jossey-Bass.

Darling-Hammond, L. (1997). *Doing what matters most: Investing in quality teaching.* New York: National Commission on Teaching and America's Future.

Darling-Hammond, L., & McLaughlin, M. (1995). Policies that support professional development in an era of reform. *Phi Delta Kappan, 76*(8), 597-604.

Elmore, R. F. (1992). Why restructuring alone won't improve teaching. *Educational Leadership, 49*(7), 44-48.

Elmore, R. (1996). Getting to scale with good educational practice. *Harvard Educational Review, 66*(1), 1-26.

Feldman, S. (1998). Bringing vitality to teaching. *Educational Leadership, 55*(5), 19-20.

Fine, M. (1994). *Charting urban school reform: Reflections on public high schools in the midst of change.* New York: Teachers College Press.

Finn, C. E., & Walberg, H. J. (1994). *Radical education reforms.* Berkeley, CA: McCutchan.

Fuhrman, S., & O'Day, J. (1996). *Rewards and reform: Creating educational incentives that work.* San Francisco: Jossey-Bass.

Fullan, M. G. (1991). *The new meaning of educational change.* New York: Teachers College Press.

Fullan, M. (1993). *Change forces: Probing the depths of educational reform.* Bristol, PA: Falmer.

Fullan, M., & Hargreaves, A. (1996). *What's worth fighting for in your school* (2nd ed.). Toronto: Ontario Public School Teachers' Federation.

Glickman, C. D. (1993). *Renewing America's schools: A guide for school-based action.* San Francisco: Jossey-Bass.

Goldring, E. B., & Rallis, S. F. (1993). *Principles of dynamic schools: Taking charge of change.* Thousand Oaks, CA: Corwin Press.

Goodlad, J. I. (1998). *Educational renewal: Better teachers, better schools* (rev. ed.). San Francisco: Jossey-Bass.

Guskey, T. R., & Huberman, M. (1990). Integrating innovations. *Educational Leadership, 47*(5), 11-15.

Guskey, T. R., & Huberman, M. (1995). *Professional development in education: New paradigms and practices.* New York: Teachers College Press.

Harvey, T. R. (1995). *Checklist for change: A pragmatic approach to creating and controlling change* (2nd ed.). Lancaster, PA: Technomic.

Herman, J., & Herman, J. L. (1994). *Making change happen: Practical planning for school leaders.* Thousand Oaks, CA: Corwin Press.

Hess, A. G. (1995). *Restructuring urban schools: A Chicago perspective.* New York: Teachers College Press.

Holmes Group. (1986). *Tomorrow's teachers.* East Lansing, MI: Author.

Holmes Group. (1990). *Tomorrow's schools.* East Lansing, MI: Author.

Holmes Group. (1995). *Tomorrow's schools of education.* East Lansing, MI: Author.

Joyce, B., & Showers, B. (1988). *Student achievement through staff development.* New York: Longman.

Lawler, E. F. (1992). *The ultimate advantage: Creating high involvement organizations.* San Francisco: Jossey-Bass.

Lieberman, A. (1995). *The work of restructuring schools: Building from the ground up.* New York: Teachers College Press.

Lieberman, A., & Miller, L. (1991). *Staff development for education in the 90's: New demands, new realities, new perspectives.* New York: Teachers College Press.

Lotto, L. S., & Thurston, P. W. (1990). *Advances in educational administration* (Vol. 1, Part A). Greenwich, CT: JAI.

Lunenburg, F. C. (1994). *Strategic planning: A manual for school administrators* (4th ed.). South Orange, NJ: Educational Consultants.

Lunenburg, F. C. (1995). *The principalship: Concepts and applications.* Englewood Cliffs, NJ: Prentice Hall.

Lunenburg, F. C., & Ornstein, A. C. (1996). *Educational administration: Concepts and practices.* Belmont, CA: Wadsworth.

Maeroff, G. I. (1993). *Team building for school change: Equipping teachers for new roles.* New York: Teachers College Press.

Marshall, G. (1993). Computer education myths and realities. In T. R. Cannings & L. Finkel (Eds.), *The technology age classroom.* Wilsonville, OR: Franklin, Beedle, & Associates.

Marzano, R. J. (1992). *A different kind of classroom: Teaching with dimensions of learning.* Alexandria, VA: Association for Supervision and Curriculum Development.

Mergendoller, J. R. (1997). Sifting the hype: What research says about technology and learning. *Principal, 76*(3), 12-14.

Mergendoller, J. R., Johnston, J., Rockman, S., & Willis, J. (1994) *Exemplary approaches to training teachers to use technology* (A report for the U.S. Office of Technology Assessment). Novato, CA: Buck Institute for Education.

Mergendoller, J. R., Sacks, C. J., & Horan, C. (1995). *The Utah educational technology initiative final evaluation: Summary of findings* (Report ETI-95-2). Novato, CA: Buck Institute for Education.

McDonald, J. P. (1996). *Redesigning school: Lessons for the 21st century.* San Francisco: Jossey-Bass.

McIntire, R. G. (1995). Characteristics of effective professional development schools. *Teacher Education and Practice, 11*(2), 41-49.

Murphy, J. (1991). *Restructuring schools: Capturing and assessing the phenomena.* New York: Teachers College Press.

National Association of Secondary School Principals. (1994). Introduction: The national alliance project for developing school leaders. *NASSP Bulletin, 78,* 1.

National Commission on Excellence in Education. (1983). *A nation at risk.* Washington, DC: Author.

National Commission on Excellence in Educational Administration. (1987). *Leaders for America's schools.* Tempe, AZ: University Council for Educational Administration.

National Commission on Teaching and America's Future. (1996). *What matters most: Teaching for America's future.* New York: Author.

National Foundation for the Improvement of Education. (1996). *Teachers take charge of their learning: Transforming professional development for student success.* Washington, DC: Author.

National Policy Board for Educational Administration. (1989). *Improving the preparation of school administrators: An agenda for reform.* Fairfax, VA: Author.

National Policy Board for Educational Administration. (1990). Focus on innovation. *Design for Leadership, 1,* 1-12.

National Policy Board for Educational Administration. (1993). *Principals for our changing schools: Knowledge and skill base.* Fairfax, VA: Author.

National Staff Development Council. (1994). *Standards for staff development.* Oxford, OH: Author.

Office of Educational Research and Improvement. (1993). *The challenge for educating teachers.* Washington, DC: Department of Education.

Office of Technology Assessment. (1995). *Teachers and technology: Making the connection.* Washington, DC: Government Printing Office.

O'Hanlon, C. (1996). *Professional development through action research: International educational perspectives.* Bristol, PA: Falmer.

Renaissance Group. (1989). *Teachers for the new world.* Cedar Falls: University of Northern Iowa.

Reynolds, A. (1996). *Summary reports of professional development school model evaluations: 1993-1996.* Fairfax, VA: George Mason University.

Rigden, D. (1996). How teachers would change teacher education. *Education Week, 16*(15), 48, 64.

Sarason, S. B. (1995). *School change: The personal development of a point of view.* New York: Teachers College Press.

Sarason, S. B. (1996). *Revisiting the culture of the school and the problem of change.* New York: Teachers College Press.

Schmuck, R. A., & Runkel, P. J. (1994). *Handbook for organization development in schools* (4th ed.). Prospect Heights, IL: Waveland.

Seashore-Louis, K. S., & Kruse, D. (Eds.). (1995). *Professionalism and community.* Thousand Oaks, CA: Corwin Press.

Shanker, A. (1996). Quality assurance: What must be done to strengthen the teaching profession. *Phi Delta Kappan, 78*(3), 224.

Sparks, D., & Hirsh, S. (1997). *The new vision for staff development.* Alexandria, VA: ASCD.

Stallings, J. A. (1991, March). *Connecting preservice teacher education and inservice professional development: A professional development school.* Paper presented at the annual meeting of the American Association of Colleges of Teacher Education, Chicago.

Stallings, J., & Kowalski, T. (1990). Research on professional development schools. In W. R. Houston (Ed.), *Handbook of research on teacher education* (pp. 251-263). New York: Macmillan.

Stover, D. (1990). Education is getting serious about administrator preparation. *Executive Educator, 12,* 18-20.

Teitel, L. (1996). *Professional development schools: A literature review.* Washington, DC: National Council for Accreditation of Teacher Education, Professional Development School Standard Project.

Wise, A., Darling-Hammond, L., & Gendler, T. (1990). *The teaching internship: Practical preparation for a licensed profession.* Santa Monica, CA: RAND.

CHAPTER **5**

Mathematics and Science Reform

By the year 2000, United States students will be first in the world in mathematics and science achievement.
(Goals 2000: Educate America Act of 1994)

There has been criticism of the U.S. educational system for over a decade. The general perception is that students in the United States are not prepared for further education or for entry into the workforce (National Commission on Excellence in Education, 1983). Although there are reports that American students score poorly in international comparisons with students from other countries in mathematics and science achievement (Dossey, Mullis, Lindquist, & Chambers, 1988; Johnston, 1987; Kirsch & Jungeblut, 1986; Lapointe, Mead, & Phillips, 1989; McKnight et al., 1987; Mullis & Jenkins, 1988; Paulos, 1988; Romberg & Stewart, 1985), one must consider the differences in what and how mathematics and science are taught in the United States and in other countries (Romberg, 1996). Nonetheless, these criticisms and the establishment of national goals have led to reform efforts in mathematics and science education (e.g., American Association for the Advancement of Science, 1989, 1993; Mathematical Association of America, 1991; Mathematical Sciences Education Board, 1989, 1990a, 1990b; National Commission, 1983; National Committee on Science Education Standards and Assessment, 1996; National

Council of Teachers of Mathematics, 1989, 1991, 1995; National Research Council, 1989; National Science Teachers Association, 1992; Secretary's Commission on Achieving Necessary Skills, 1991).

Research: The School Mathematics Reform Movement

The curriculum and evaluation standards of the National Council of Teachers of Mathematics (1989) and the national science education standards developed by the National Committee on Science Education Standards and Assessment (1996) are focused on mathematical and science literacy for all students: classroom instruction based on exploration and inquiry, assessment practices aligned with the curriculum, and recommendations for change in the way teachers are prepared.

The curriculum and evaluation standards for school mathematics were formulated to build a foundation for all students to gain access to a comprehensive mathematics program throughout their schooling (National Council, 1989; see Box 5.1).

When compared to the National Council of Teachers of Mathematics's (NCTM) five goals for students, the mathematics curriculum in many of today's schools is inadequate. The new curriculum standards (National Council, 1989) point to the need to change the whole environment for learning: changes in what is taught, how it is taught, and how it is assessed.

The Mathematics Standards

The foregoing concepts lay at the heart of NCTM's work to develop the standards. There are 40 curriculum standards divided by grade level—K-4, 5-8, and 9-12—and a comprehensive set of 14 evaluation standards.

Unique to the construction of the standards is the concept of mathematics as an integrated whole, kindergarten through 12th grade, rather than mathematics as a collection of individual topics isolated by grade levels. For example, algebraic and geometric concepts are developed even in the earliest grades, where teachers help children explore, reason, and infer with patterns and shapes as a way of avoiding the later shock of the formal—and often formidable—secondary school courses.

Box 5.1. Five Goals of the NCTM Mathematics Standards

Students should

1. *Learn to value mathematics.* Students should have numerous, varied learning experiences that illuminate the cultural, historical, and scientific evolution of mathematics. These experiences should be designed to evoke students' appreciation of mathematics' role in the development of contemporary society and to promote their understanding of relationships among the fields of mathematics and the disciplines they serve: the humanities and the physical, social, and life sciences.

2. *Learn to reason mathematically.* Today's students will live and work in the 21st century, an era dominated by computers and by a global economy. Jobs that contribute to such an economy will require workers who are prepared to internalize new ideas, to perceive patterns, and to solve complex problems. Hence, students of mathematics must learn to gather evidence, to make conjectures, to formulate models, and to develop arguments to support a theory. Therefore, sound reasoning should be promoted as much as students' ability to find correct answers.

3. *Learn to communicate mathematically.* Students need to learn the symbols and terms of mathematics to express and expand their understanding of mathematical ideas. This goal is

For each grade-level group—K-4, 5-8, and 9-12—the curriculum content emphasizes opportunities for students to develop an understanding of mathematical models and structures. Within each group, each standard is rooted in certain assumptions, the most prominent of which is that *knowing* mathematics is *doing* mathematics. The format for all the standards is the same: Each one identifies the topic; indicates student activities; develops the rationale; and gives examples, materials, and instructional strategies.

The first three standards cut across all grade levels: mathematics as problem solving, mathematics as communication, and mathematics as reasoning. Mathematical connections, the fourth curriculum standard, is the connecting link showing how mathematics is related both across mathematical topics and across other disciplines.

best accomplished in the context of problem solving: students working in groups, teaching one another, arguing about strategies, and expressing arguments carefully in writing.

4. *Become mathematical problem solvers.* Today's workplace expects graduates to be able to use a wide variety of mathematical methods to solve problems. Students of mathematics must experience a variety of problems during schoolwork. They must lean to analyze problems, to select strategies for solving problems, to formulate several solutions to problems, and to work with others in reaching consensus on solutions. Problem-solving tools, including calculators, computers, coursework, and manipulatives, are necessary for conceptual development in mathematics.

5. *Become confident in their mathematical abilities.* In our technological age, mathematics has, of necessity, permeated the home and the workplace of every citizen. The ability to cope with the demands of everyday life depends on the attitudes students develop toward mathematics during school experiences. A variety of experiences "doing" mathematics outside of school as well as in school develops trust in students' thinking skills and their growing mathematical power.

SOURCE: National Council of Teachers of Mathematics (1989).

Guided by these four common standards, sustained developmentally throughout the K-12 continuum, students can experience the power, beauty, and usefulness of mathematics. Nine or 10 additional topical standards are also given for each grade-level group.

Fourteen evaluation standards and new methods of assessment accompany these curricular changes in context, content, and method. The evaluation standards are divided into three categories: The first comprises general assessment strategies for the curriculum.

The second category, student assessment, contains seven standards intended to give feedback to teachers both on the effectiveness of their instruction and on students' mathematical progress.

The third category—program evaluation—provides help in the evaluation of programs and instruction; offers alternative methods of

Box 5.2. Assumptions of Mathematics Reform

Mathematics is something a person does. Knowing mathematics means being able to use it in meaningful ways. To learn mathematics, students must be engaged in exploring, conjecturing, and thinking rather than only in rote learning of rules and procedures. When students construct their own personal knowledge derived from meaningful experiences, they will more readily retain and use what they have learned. This underlies teachers' new role in providing learning experiences that help students make sense of mathematics and to view and use it as a tool for reasoning and problem solving.

Mathematics has broad content encompassing many fields. Because technology has affected the use of technology in the home and the workplace, the mathematical sciences are no longer a requirement for future scientists alone. Mathematics has become an essential component in the education of all Americans. In other words, mathematics is more powerful than ever before because the discipline is being enhanced by new results from applied fields. Students can benefit from exposure to a broad range of content that reveals the utility of mathematics, through which students can build on understanding of the place of mathematics in a technological society.

assessment to reflect the diversity, scope, and intent of NCTM's vision of school mathematics; and guides and supports change (National Council, 1989).

The changes presented in the standards have influenced curriculum and instruction in many schools. What has emerged during the past 9 years is a new description of mathematical proficiency. The definition of mathematical proficiency has expanded to include frequent use of terms such as *reasoning, communication, problem solving, conceptual understanding, mathematical power,* and *authentic assessment.* These changes are based on the underlying assumptions about students, mathematics, and students learning presented in Box 5.2.

Mathematics instruction and learning can be improved through appropriate evaluation. Evaluation should be an integral part of teaching and learning about mathematics. Evaluation should concentrate on assessing what students know, how they reason, and how they feel about mathematics. If teachers want students to investigate, explore, and discover, assessment must not measure just rote memory but understanding and the ability to tie new knowledge to existing knowledge.

Mathematical power can—and must—be at the command of all students in a technological society. With proper instruction, students can gain the necessary confidence, knowledge, and techniques for applying mathematics to everyday problems. The challenge of what is proper in the delivery of instruction comes with continuous professional development for the teachers, not with administrative directives. The more sophisticated the teacher in the integration of mathematics and technology, the more likely the students will learn. Students can develop strategies for continuing to learn and use mathematics with confidence as the world about them continually changes.

SOURCE: National Council of Teachers of Mathematics (1989).

Research: The School Science Reform Movement

This nation has established a goal that all students should achieve scientific literacy. The national science education standards (National Committee, 1996) are designed to enable the nation to achieve that goal. They outline what students need to know and be able to do to be scientifically literate at different grade levels. They describe an educational system in which all students demonstrate high levels of performance, in which teachers decide what is essential for effective learning, and in which supportive programs nurture achievement.

In the 1980s, the American Chemical Society, the Biological Sciences Curriculum Study, the Education Development Center, the National Science Resources Center, and the Technical Education Resources Center all developed innovative science curricula. The American Association for the Advancement of Science published *Science for All Americans* in 1989 and *Benchmarks for Science Literacy* in 1993. In 1992, the National Science Teachers Association, through its Scope, Sequence, and Coordination Project, published *The Content Core.*

The many individuals who developed the content standards sections of the national science education standards, one of six sections of the standards, acknowledge their indebtedness to the seminal work by the American Association for the Advancement of Science's *Science for All Americans* (1989) and *Benchmarks for Science Literacy* (1993). The standards made independent use and interpretation of the statements contained in these two documents of what all students should know and be able to do.

The Science Standards

The national science education standards are organized into six sections: standards for science teaching, standards for professional development of science teachers, standards for assessment in science education, standards for science content, standards for science education programs, and standards for science education systems.

The standards for science teaching focus on what teachers know and do. The standards for the professional development of teachers focus on how teachers develop professional knowledge and skill. Together, these standards present a broad and deep view of science teaching that is based on the conviction that scientific inquiry is at the heart of science and science learning.

The science education assessment standards are criteria for judging the quality of assessment practices. The assessment standards are also designed to be used as guides in developing assessment practices and policy. These standards apply equally to classroom-based and externally designed assessments and to formative and summative assessments.

The content standards are organized by K-4, 5-8, and 9-12 grade levels. These standards provide expectations for the development of student understanding and ability over the course of K-12 education. Content is defined to include inquiry; the traditional subject areas of physical, life, and earth and space sciences; connections between science and technology; science in personal and social perspectives; and the history and nature of science. The content standards are supplemented with information on developing student understanding, and they include fundamental concepts that underlie each standard.

The program standards provide criteria for judging the quality of school and district science programs. The program standards focus on issues that relate to opportunities for students to learn and for teachers to teach science.

The system standards consist of criteria for judging the performance of components of the science education system beyond the school and district: the people and entities, including education professionals and the broader community that supports the schools.

Throughout the standards, examples are based on actual practice. These examples demonstrate that the vision is attainable. Each example includes a brief description of some of its features and lists the standards that might be highlighted by the example. Many of the examples are appropriate only if students have been involved in the type of science education described in the standards. For instance, the assessment exercises are appropriate if students have had the opportunity to gain the understanding and skills being assessed (National Committee, 1996).

Applying Research to Practice: Developing an Action Plan

Strategy 1: Develop Curriculum that Integrates Science and Mathematics

School leaders should consider interdisciplinary teamwork for the development of integrated science and mathematics. They may draw from current models, research, and science and mathematics education reform documents such as that by Donna Berlin and Arthur White (1995), who define three broad domains of education: integrated school science and mathematics, assessment, and technology. These authors provide a list of characteristics to guide in the development of assessment for integrated school science and mathematics using technology. Their goal is to connect science, mathematics, instruction,

Box 5.3. Principles of Science Reform

Science for all students. The standards assume the inclusion of all students, regardless of age, gender, cultural or ethnic background, disabilities, or interest, in challenging science learning opportunities and defining levels of understanding and abilities that all should develop. Resources must be allocated to ensure that the standards do not exacerbate the differences in opportunities to learn that currently exist between advantaged and disadvantaged students.

Learning science is an active process. In learning science, students engage in inquiry-oriented investigations in which they interact with their teachers and peers. Students establish connections between their current knowledge of science and the scientific knowledge found in many sources; they apply science content to new questions; they engage in problem solving, planning, decision making, and group discussions; and they experience authentic assessments consistent with an active learning approach.

School science reflects the intellectual and cultural traditions that characterize the practice of contemporary science. To develop a knowledge of science, students must become familiar

assessment, and technology so as to enrich the teaching-learning process and accurately determine the outcomes of this process.

The National Committee on Science Education Standards and Assessment (1996) outlines four categories of science content standards: science as inquiry, science subject matter, scientific connections, and science and human affairs. The "connection of sciences with mathematics" is explicitly mentioned in the scientific connections category. Similarly, the National Council of Teachers of Mathematics (1989) suggests a comparable position. For grades K-4, 5-8, and 9-12, respectively, "instructional practices characterized by content integration" (p. 20), "connecting mathematics to other subjects and to the world outside the classroom" (p. 70), and "the use of real-world problems to motivate and apply theory" (p. 126) are recommended.

with modes of scientific inquiry, rules of evidence, ways of formulating questions, and ways of proposing explanations. The understanding of the nature of science, science subject matter, and the relation of science to mathematics and to technology should also be part of student's science education.

Improving science education is part of systemic education reform. National goals and standards contribute to state and local systemic reform, which complement each other. Science education is a subsystem of the larger education system. The components of the larger education system include classrooms, schools, and school districts; parents; teacher education programs in colleges and universities; textbooks and textbook publishers; scientists and engineers; science museums; business and industry; and legislators. The national science education standards provide the unity of purpose and vision required to focus the aforementioned components effectively on the important task of improving science education for all students.

SOURCE: National Committee on Science Education Standards and Assessment (1996).

Support for integration is often couched in the context of constructivist (Brooks & Brooks, 1993; Hyerle, 1996; Marzano, 1992; Steffe & Gale, 1994) and neuropsychological (Hamilton & Ghatala, 1994; Krupnik-Gottlieb & Berlin, 1994) learning theory. Although these theories are often put forth as a rationale for integrated school science and mathematics, there is little research to document the benefits of such integration (Berlin, 1991).

A Suggested Model

The Berlin-White Integrated Science and Mathematics Model (BWISM) was developed in an attempt to remedy that situation. The BWISM identifies six aspects: ways of learning, ways of knowing, process and thinking skills, content knowledge, attitudes and perceptions, and teaching strategies (Berlin & White, 1994).

Ways of Learning. To integrate science and mathematics, students need to be actively involved in a learning environment that encourages pattern seeking, the exploration of big ideas, and the interrelationships between concepts and processes.

Ways of Knowing. Integrated science and mathematics activities can provide opportunities to move back and forth between the inductive and deductive ways of knowing. According to Berlin and White (1994), induction is described as the process of looking at numerous examples to find a pattern that can then be translated into a rule. The application of this rule in a new context is the process of deduction. The process of induction can then provide the empirical verification of the rule. If the rule is not verified, new patterns are sought and a modified or new rule is generated (induction).

Process and Thinking Skills. Integration of science and mathematics involves data collection and use, experimentation, and problem solving. Skills such as collecting, classifying, and organizing data; controlling variables; developing models; making hypothesis; patterning; and interpreting data are examples of this aspect.

Content Knowledge. The examination of concepts, principles, and theories of science and mathematics may reveal ideas unique and overlapping in each discipline. Thus, science and mathematics disciplines can be integrated in areas in which the content overlaps in the two disciplines.

Attitudes and Perceptions. Similar values and ways of thinking are shared by science and mathematics, including basing decisions on data, skepticism, logical reasoning, and consideration of other explanations.

Teaching Strategies. Integrated science and mathematics should include broad content, inquiry-based learning, laboratory experiments, the use of technology, and facilitation of connections between science and mathematics. If science is integrated in current curricula, then cautions must be taken to make certain that the content and process knowledge are maintained (Irby, 1996).

Strategy 2: Develop a Plan for Science and Mathematics Assessment

Both mathematics education and science education documents recommend assessment characteristics in mathematics and science teaching; therefore, it is critical that school leaders develop an effective assessment plan for their schools. The National Council of Teachers of Mathematics (1995) suggests that assessment should be an integral, routine part of the teaching and learning that takes place in classrooms as a means to enhance mathematics learning. Put another way, "curriculum, instruction, and assessment are three interrelated parts of a single process aimed at developing students' mathematical power" (p. 35). Similarly, the National Committee on Science Education Standards and Assessment (1996) recognizes the interdependence of curriculum, instruction, and assessment. Content, teaching, and assessment standards were developed concurrently so that teaching and assessment practices would be consistent with content.

According to Berlin and White (1995), this alignment can be achieved through the use of performance-based or embedded assessments. Performance tasks have been developed as a way to coordinate among curriculum, instruction, and assessment. They can serve as a means to assess conceptual knowledge, determine the level of understanding, integrate knowledge across disciplines, assess higher-order thinking skills, monitor thinking processes, and enhance motivation through relevant teaching environments (National Committee, 1996).

Strategy 3: Integrate Technology with Mathematics and Science Education

With the advancement of technology into both curriculum and instruction apparent in current mathematics and science education reform documents, school leaders will need to consider technology as an integrated part of the curriculum. Because technology is changing mathematics and its uses—we believe that appropriate calculators should be available to all students at all times; a computer should be available in every classroom for demonstration purposes; every student should have access to a computer for individual and group work; students should learn to use the computer as a tool for processing information and performing calculations to investigate and solve problems (National Council, 1989).

Technology can be useful for identifying connections among various mathematical topics. "Because the computer allows students to enter countless values and immediately see the resulting geometric shape, they might find it both interesting and rewarding to investigate interrelationships between number and geometry" (National Council, 1989, p. 85). Technology is also recognized as an important connection in the school science content (National Committee, 1996).

The role of technology has been specifically addressed in the *Assessment Standards for School Mathematics* (National Council, 1995) and the *National Science Education Standards* (National Committee, 1996). Technology can be used as a delivery system, context (i.e., real-world, problem solving and inquiry), monitor, or manager for assessment. Some of the exciting technology-based assessments include recording observation and interview notes on electronic pads; scanning student work for portfolios; software programs that monitor and record work; tests and quizzes that are electronically administered, scored, modified, and recorded; and the generation of multidimensional, graphics-based student profiles. "The potential impact of the variety of new electronic tools for the development of new assessment systems has yet to be tapped" (National Council, 1995, p. 229).

The BWISM can serve as a template for integrated school science and mathematics, assessment, and technology (Berlin & White, 1987). The following characteristics can guide in the development of assessment for integrated school science and mathematics that can use the potential of technology:

- Engage students in problem solving.
- Engage students in inquiry.
- Invoke real-world applications and contextualized problems.
- Use performance-based tasks.
- Use tasks embedded within instruction.
- Use appropriate technology.
- Provide for multimodal experiences and opportunities for modal translations.

- Provide opportunities for communication, collaboration, and socialization.
- Encourage multiple modes of expression.
- Encourage higher-order thinking skills.
- Reveal conceptual knowledge.
- Reveal procedural knowledge.
- Reveal student processing and reasoning.
- Recognize student attitudes and perceptions. (Berlin & White, 1995, p. 53)

Educational leaders in schools can integrate Goal 5 with Goal 3 and double the influence in mathematics and science reform.

References

American Association for the Advancement of Science. (1989). *Science for all Americans*. New York: Oxford University Press.

American Association for the Advancement of Science. (1993). *Benchmarks for science literacy*. New York: Oxford University Press.

Berlin, D. F. (1991). *Integrating science and mathematics: A bibliography* (School Science and Mathematics Association Topics for Teachers Series, No. 6). Columbus, OH: ERIC Clearinghouse for Science, Mathematics, and Environmental Education.

Berlin, D. F., & White, A. L. (1987). An instructional model for integrating the calculator. *Arithmetic Teacher, 34*(6), 52-54.

Berlin, D. F., & White, A. L. (1994). The Berlin-White integrated science and mathematics model. *School Science and Mathematics, 94*(1), 2-4.

Berlin, D. F., & White, A. L. (1995). Using technology in assessing integrated science and mathematics learning. *Journal of Science Education and Technology, 4*(1), 47-56.

Brooks, J. G., & Brooks, M. G. (1993). *In search of understanding: The case for constructivist classrooms*. Alexandria, VA: Association for Supervision and Curriculum Development.

Dossey, J. A., Mullis, I. V. S., Lindquist, M. M., & Chambers, D. L. (1988). *The mathematics report card: Are we measuring up? Trends and achievement based on 1986 national assessment*. Princeton, NJ: Educational Testing Service.

Hamilton, R., & Ghatala, E. (1994). *Learning and instruction.* New York: McGraw-Hill.

Hyerle, D. (1996). *Visual tools for constructing knowledge.* Alexandria, VA: Association for Supervision and Curriculum Development.

Irby, B. J. (1996, October). *Increasing higher order thinking skills among bilingual students.* Paper presented to the Cypress-Fairbanks Independent School District, Houston, TX.

Johnston, W. B. (1987). *Workforce 2000: Work and workers for the twenty-first century.* Croton-on-Hudson, NY: Hudson Institute.

Kirsch, I. S., & Jungeblut, A. (1986). *Literacy profiles of America's young adults.* Princeton, NJ: Educational Testing Service.

Krupnik-Gottlieb, M., & Berlin, D. F. (1994). *Integration with the brain in mind.* Unpublished manuscript, The National Center for Science Teaching and Learning, Ohio State University, Columbus.

Lapointe, A. E., Mead, N. A., & Phillips, G. W. (1989). *A world of difference: An international assessment of science and mathematics.* Princeton, NJ: Educational Testing Service.

Marzano, R. J. (1992). *A different kind of classroom: Teaching with dimensions of learning.* Alexandria, VA: Association for Supervision and Curriculum Development.

Mathematical Association of America. (1991). *A call for change: Recommendations for the mathematical preparation of teachers.* Washington, DC: Author.

Mathematical Sciences Education Board. (1989). *Everybody counts.* Washington, DC: Author.

Mathematical Sciences Education Board. (1990a). *On the shoulders of giants.* Washington, DC: Author.

Mathematical Sciences Education Board. (1990b). *Shaping school mathematics: A philosophy and framework for curriculum.* Washington, DC: Author.

McKnight, C. C., Crosswhite, F. J., Dossey, J. A., Kifer, E., Swafford, J. O., Travers, K. J., & Cooney, T. J. (1987). *The underachieving curriculum: Assessing U.S. school mathematics from an international perspective.* Champaign, IL: Stipes.

Mullis, I. V. S., & Jenkins, L. B. (1988). *The science report card: Elements of risk and recovery.* Princeton, NJ: Educational Testing Service.

National Commission on Excellence in Education. (1983). *A nation at risk.* Washington, DC: Government Printing Office.

National Committee on Science Education Standards and Assessment. (1996). *National science education standards.* Washington, DC: National Academy Press.

National Council of Teachers of Mathematics. (1989). *Curriculum and evaluation standards for school mathematics.* Reston, VA: Author.

National Council of Teachers of Mathematics. (1991). *Professional standards for teaching mathematics.* Reston, VA: Author.

National Council of Teachers of Mathematics. (1995). *Assessment standards for school mathematics.* Reston, VA: Author.

National Research Council. (1989). *Everybody counts: A report to the nation of the future of mathematics education.* Washington, DC: National Academy Press.

National Science Teachers Association. (1992). *Scope, sequence, and coordinating of secondary school science: Vol. 1. The content core: A guide for curriculum developers.* Washington, DC: Author.

Paulos, J. A. (1988). *Innumeracy: Mathematics illiteracy and its consequences.* New York: Hill & Wang.

Romberg, T. A. (1996). Problematic features of the school mathematics curriculum. In P. Jackson (Ed.), *Handbook of research on curriculum.* New York: Simon & Schuster.

Romberg, T. A., & Stewart, D. M. (1985). *School mathematics: Options for the 1990s, proceedings of the conference.* Madison, WI: Office of Research and Educational Improvement.

Secretary's Commission on Achieving Necessary Skills. (1991). *What work requires of schools.* Washington, DC: Government Printing Office.

Steffe, L. P., & Gale, J. (1994). *Constructivism in education.* Hillsdale, NJ: Lawrence Erlbaum.

CHAPTER 6

Every Adult Literate

By the year 2000, every adult American will be literate and will possess the knowledge and skills necessary to compete in a global economy and exercise the rights and responsibilities of citizenship.

(Goals 2000: Educate America Act of 1994)

Twenty-one to 23%, or 40 to 44 million, U.S. citizens between 21 and 25 years old scored at Level 1 on the National Adult Literacy Survey (Kirsch, Jungeblut, Jenkins, & Kolstad, 1993). Their literacy skills ranged from having almost no reading, writing, or quantitative skills to being able to total an entry on a bank deposit slip or locate the time or place of a meeting on a form (Fagan, 1995).

Research: Adult Literacy

"The National Adult Literacy Survey (NALS) was used to fill the need for accurate and detailed information on the English literacy skills of America's adults" (Kirsch et al., 1993, p. 1). NALS measures one of five levels of literacy proficiency across three scales: prose, document, and quantitative. The prose scale measures the knowledge and skills needed to understand and use information from texts that include editorials, news stories, poems, and fiction. The document scale measures the knowledge and skills required to locate and use information contained in materials that include job applications, payroll forms, and bus schedules. The quantitative scale measures the knowledge and skills required to apply arithmetic operations, either alone or sequentially, using numbers embedded in printed materials such as balancing a checkbook, figuring out a tip, and completing an order form. Level 1 is the lowest level of literacy proficiency and Level 5 is the highest.

What does it mean that 21% to 23%, or 40 to 44 million, adults scored at Level 1 on NALS? Such surveys keep the issue of adult literacy visible. They also provide elaborate databases that may be useful for particular stakeholders: government, business, education, and literacy agencies. Kirsch et al. (1993) caution, however, about the applicability of the results to real-life situations: "Because it is impossible to say precisely what literacy skills are essential to succeed in this or any other society, the results of the National Adult Literacy Survey provide no firm answers to such questions" (p. xviii).

Policymakers and other education stakeholders concerned about reducing the dropout rate and increasing school success for all students need to consider the parents' literacy levels, or they will be ignoring an important aspect of the school success equation. Recognition of the intergenerational role that parents play as family educators places a much higher premium on the importance of adult literacy programs than has been accorded previously.

Applying Research to Practice: Developing an Action Plan

Strategy 1: Develop an Adult Literacy Program

Many schools and municipalities operate adult literacy programs. Some are open to the general public, whereas others are designed to target specific populations. Some seek external funding through grants or foundations. Many receive some federal funding administered through their state government. In most states, federal adult literacy funds are administered by three agencies: the state department of education; the governor's office; and coordinated efforts of departments of corrections, social services, vocational schools, community

(text continues on p. 114)

Box 6.1. What the Research Says About . . .

The Labor Force

- Reports and studies of the past decade (Commission on the Skills, 1990; National Commission, 1983) point to the high numbers of American workers entering the labor force without the requisite academic and work-related skills needed to succeed in an increasingly competitive workforce (Ananda, Rabinowitz, Carlos, & Yamashiro, 1995).

- In 1994, the federal government passed three interlocking pieces of legislation: the School-to-Work Opportunities Act, the Improving America's Schools Act, and Goals 2000: The Educate America Act that jointly promote the development of systems of national academic and industry skill standards.

Adult Literacy

- Most government agencies define a literate adult as one who has achieved a ninth-grade, eighth-grade, seventh-grade, or fourth-grade reading level (Kirsch et al., 1993).

- Some researchers designate a person who has basic survival skills as being functionally literate. At the lowest level, this may include the ability to distinguish—on a grocery shelf—between a lemon-scented dishwashing detergent (with a lemon on the label) and lemon juice. At a higher level, functional literacy is the ability to fill out a job, food stamp, or unemployment application. Although it is important that all American citizens have these minimal skills, literacy encompasses far more (Ellsworth, Hedley, & Baratta, 1994; Kirsch et al., 1993).

- The National Adult Literacy Survey (NALS) defines literacy as "using printed and written information to function in society, to achieve one's goals, and to develop one's knowledge potential" (Kirsch et al., 1993, p.2).

- The National Assessment of Educational Progress (NAEP) has conducted the most thorough research to date on literacy levels across all age groups. NAEP defines literacy within three broad categories: prose (information from texts), document (application forms, maps), and quantitative (using numbers), which are similar to the NALS scales (Kirsch et al., 1993).

◆ Supervisors in six manufacturing companies report that adult literacy programs resulted in improvements in job training, job performance, promotability of participants, and productivity, such as scrap reduction, reduced paperwork, and less wastage (Lehr & Osborn, 1994).

◆ Other research found that more literate workers, who use their literacy skills on the job, may increase their productivity as much as 10% to 15% (Gowen, 1992).

Literacy and Social Issues

◆ Researchers at the University of Pennsylvania found that companies increasing the educational level of their workforce by 1 year experienced an 8.6% increase in productivity (Hirsch & Mortensen, 1996).

◆ Low levels of literacy bear a relationship to several social problems such as poverty, unemployment, crime, homelessness, and drug abuse. A study of welfare recipients found that more than 85% had held jobs at one time or another but often for only brief periods (New Jersey Welfare Department, 1996). The study also points out that nearly half of welfare recipients return to welfare, which suggests that many fail to make a successful transition to self-sufficiency. Those with a high school education were far more likely to be working and self-sufficient than those who had not finished high school. The National Bureau of Economic Research (1996) found that each additional year of school beyond high school yields approximately an 8% to 9% increase in salary annually.

◆ Adults lacking a high school diploma constitute about 25% of persons seeking employment through a state employment agency (Wisconsin State Employment Service, 1996). A state library study found that these individuals are twice as likely to live below the poverty level; are more likely to be unemployed; are in households earning roughly three fourths the pay earned by more literate households; and are more likely to live in rural than in urban areas of the country (Indiana State Library Association, 1997).

(continued)

Box 6.1. Continued

◆ Several studies have found a link between crime and low literacy levels. One study found that a high percentage of delinquent boys suffered from undiagnosed learning disabilities. After receiving remedial education, few repeated subsequent crimes (Soifer et al., 1990). Hodgkinson (1995) found a high correlation between states that had a high dropout rate and those with high prison populations. Nearly 100% of probationers who lack a high school diploma or General Equivalency Diploma are chronically unemployed or underemployed. Sixty percent of probationers have low literacy levels. There is an inverse relationship between increased literacy and problems with violence. As adults become more educated, they take time to think about their actions.

◆ Evidence shows a relationship between low literacy levels and homelessness and substance abuse. Homelessness can be traced to unemployment due to poor work-related skills, which is exacerbated by the inability to complete forms for government assistance: unemployment, welfare assistance, food stamps, and the like. Low self-esteem, which is associated with low reading levels, can lead to substance abuse and antisocial behavior such as battery and neurotic disorders.

Family Literacy

◆ The family literacy concept recognizes the family as an institution for education and the role of parents as their children's first teacher (Sticht, 1995).

◆ Parents with higher literacy levels spend more time with their children talking about school, helping them with their homework, taking them to the library, and reading to them than parents with lower literacy levels. Furthermore, better educated parents spend more time going to and helping with school activities; they talk more with teachers about their children's education; and their children attend school more and show improvements in their school grades, test scores, and reading and mathematics achievement. Children of lesser educated parents score significantly lower in both reading comprehension and mathematics from the fifth grade on, when marginally literate parents can no longer assist with homework. Moreover, parents with low basic skills are intimidated by their children's school. They are less likely to attend parent conferences and may be unable to read notes from the teacher.

◆ Better educated parents send children to school better prepared to learn, with higher levels of language skills and knowledge about books and other literacy tools needed for school and life. Better educated mothers have healthier babies, smaller families, children better prepared to start school, and children who stay in school and learn more.

Today's Employees

◆ Today's workplace needs employees who can take on greater responsibility, collaborate effectively, become more involved in decision-making processes, and resolve unforeseen problems (Commission on the Skills of the American Workforce, 1990; Council of Chief State School Officers, 1995; Secretary's Commission on Achieving Necessary Skills, 1991).

◆ A study by the Department of Labor (1991) found that employers wanted their employees to have interpersonal skills, the ability to reason and to solve problems, and the ability to perform a variety of tasks, in addition to competence in the basic skills of reading, writing, and computation.

◆ UNISYS has spent over $1 million on color photos that depict how machines are to be assembled because many workers have difficulty with narrative descriptions in technical manuals (UNISYS, 1996).

colleges, and universities. Funds channeled to municipalities that operate adult literacy programs are administered by city agencies analogous to state government. One action for school leaders to take is to
review other programs in municipalities or schools that conduct adult
literacy programs.

Example 1: The New York City
Adult Literacy Initiative

The New York City Adult Literacy Initiative, coordinated by the
New York City Mayor's Office of Education Services and the New
York State Education Department, offers a range of programs to a
diverse population. The programs are provided through a network of
literacy provider agencies—the New York City Board of Education,
the Community Development Agency, the City University of New
York, and the public libraries of Manhattan, Queens, and Brooklyn.
Programs are conducted in all five boroughs of New York City and take
place at 14 college campuses; more than 175 board of education sites
(public schools, community organizations, and unions); 24 branch
libraries; and 40 community-based organizations that combine literacy instruction with social services and community support (Literacy
Assistance Center, 1990).

The initiative program has become one of the largest in the nation.
It is now recognized as a national model for both its range of services
for adult learners and its high level of coordination. The strength of
the initiative is in its ability to meet the needs of such a diverse population and provide these students with an environment in which they
can flourish.

The majority of the initiative's students are enrolled in basic education (BE), English for speakers of other languages (ESOL), and
basic education in the native language (BENL). In 1988-1989, students in BE (39.3%) and ESOL (56.9%) made up 96% of the student
population; the remaining 4% were enrolled in BENL classes.

BE instruction is aimed at improving reading and writing skills for
adults testing below the ninth-grade level on a standardized test.
ESOL instruction is designed to improve speaking skills and listening
comprehension in English. Most often, the emphasis is on spoken
rather than written language. Increasingly, though, students' writings
are used as a tool in language development. BENL instruction aims to
improve the reading and writing skills of adults in their native lan-

guage. It targets adults performing below the ninth-grade level on a standardized test.

The BE and ESOL programs are further broken down into four instructional levels. In BE, the four levels are determined by performance on a standardized test, the Test of Adult Basic English (TABE). In ESOL, student placement in the four levels is determined by an individually administered oral/aural exam (the John Test). Furthermore, the initiative's guidelines recommend that adult learners in the two lower levels of BE and ESOL make up half of the student population in literacy programs. The initiative remains committed to attracting and serving this population most in need.

Recently, the initiative has extended its reach and adapted its form to provide literacy instruction in cooperation with other social service programs, such as drug rehabilitation programs; services for ex-offenders and youth in trouble with the law; special services for youth—vocational, artistic, and health; and services for refugees and recent immigrants.

Literacy and Employment. A major goal of the initiative is to improve the employment outlook for New York City residents. Initiative programs provide general employment readiness training and vocational counseling to many adult learners. Instructors often employ materials relating to the everyday tasks that workers perform at their jobs. In a special workplace literacy program, classes are held at the work site.

Adults who attend literacy programs are motivated very often by a desire to find employment, improve their performance in their current occupations, attain promotions or new jobs, or begin a career. The initiative works hard at reaching adults who are not employed and strives to prepare them for the increasingly sophisticated job demands of the present day.

During program year 1988-89, nearly 2,000 adults reported obtaining a job; another 800 adults reported getting a better job; and approximately 500 adults reported either removing themselves from public assistance or reducing the amount they received. These figures underrepresent the total, because the data monitored by the Literacy Assistance Center are dependent on students reporting information to the initiative.

Achievement. When students enter the initiative, they are given a test to assess their levels of literacy abilities. The test is used to determine class placement and to provide a baseline that can be used later to document students' progress. The standard instruments used are the TABE for students enrolled in basic education and the John Test for those enrolled in English for speakers of other languages. An improvement of 0.5 or more in grade level constitutes gain on the TABE; an increase of 10 points or more on the John Test is considered gain.

A number of adults have obtained jobs or gotten better jobs while enrolled in literacy programs. Other examples of achievement, as reported by students, during the 1988-89 program year are as follows: Nearly 900 adults advanced from BE classes to high school equivalency classes leading to a General Equivalency Diploma (GED); another 1,600 adult learners obtained a GED; an additional 1,300 adults entered other educational programs; and approximately 2,000 students registered to vote.

Cost. The New York City Adult Literacy Initiative served approximately 50,000 adult learners during 1988-89. Nearly two thirds of the initiative's students were female, whereas just over one third were male; almost 4 out of 5 adult learners were either Hispanic or black; and nearly 3 out of 5 students were between the ages of 25 and 44. This represents only a small percentage of New York City's adults with nonfunctional literacy skills; the number served is perhaps as low as 3% of those eligible. A similarly small percentage is being reached state- and nationwide.

During the 1988-89 program year, the state and city provided approximately $31.2 million to programs offering free literacy services to adults. Of this sum, $21.2 million was allocated directly to providing instructional services at City University campuses, community-based organizations, and board of education sites. For these programs, the average cost per instructional hour was $53; the average cost per contact hour was $4; and the average cost per student was $434.

An additional $2.6 million was allocated to the three public library systems, which provide small group and individual tutorial instruction, computer-assisted instruction, and study tables, as well as space and both print and audio-visual materials (including sets of instructional materials) for use by other literacy programs.

The remaining funds were used for a wide range of support and administrative services provided by the literacy provider agencies and the Literacy Assistance Center. Among the initiative-wide services were staff development, program oversight and technical assistance, counselor training, data processing and analysis, referral services, and special projects of various kinds.

Example 2: Bringing Non-English Speaking
Families Into the Community of the School

Another exemplary literacy program that addresses the growing diversity of our country and infuses technology can be found in the rural area of Lowes, Kentucky, at Lowes Elementary School, Graves County Schools. Graves County is focusing Goals 2000 resources on non-English speaking families in the Lowes community, with the objective of increasing their involvement in the schools and reducing the high dropout rate of non-English speaking students. Technology assists in this process as a tool for the family to increase bilingual skills, to communicate with others of their own ethnicity through e-mail, and to communicate more easily with the English-speaking community. In addition, students enrolled in advanced Spanish language classes and their teachers benefit from increased involvement with this special population.

Non-English-speaking parents are invited to school at least once each week to use computers to increase their bilingual and job skills. High school students accompany their Spanish teacher to the elementary school once or twice each week to communicate in Spanish and English with the Spanish-speaking students. High school students assist Spanish-speaking students and their parents with computer knowledge and learning how the computer can be used by a family. Finally, high school students accompany a Spanish-speaking adult to one or more community or civic functions to translate and ensure that the adult understands what transpired and how to participate.

Seaboard Farms joined the school district as a partner in this project and provides Spanish- and English-speaking employees to emphasize the value of technology skills in the workplace. All Spanish-speaking family members are provided the opportunity to learn English as a second language in a school setting supported by technology loaned to the home. Critical basic life skills, such as communicating well in supermarkets, with doctors, and with the school, are stressed. Family Resource Centers also involve families to assist them in their acculturation to the United States (Lowes Elementary, Graves County Schools, 1997).

**Strategy 2: Establish an Agenda
for Lifelong Learning**

The action agenda for lifelong learning for the 21st century, an outcome of the First Global Conference on Lifelong Learning held in Rome, Italy, in 1995, contains a range of challenges and recommendations addressed to individuals, organizations, business, educational institutions, universities, governments, and the media (Ball, 1995). This is a recommendation for action that school leaders should promote in their communities. Following are suggestions and challenges that need to be addressed in the next few years.

Individuals

Individuals should each take responsibility for their own learning and write down a personal learning plan (PLP) and keep a learning passport (LP); invite a friend or colleague to act as mentor; encourage others to develop their PLPs and LPs; and offer to act as guide or mentor for others.

Organizations

Organizations should each make a commitment to become a learning organization and establish a shared mission statement, including a commitment to lifelong learning; identify the learning process as a major business process aligned with the organization's mission and objectives; benchmark performance against best practice; and explore the possibilities of publishing the "missing balance sheet" of human resources in terms of the achievement of, and potential for, learning.

Business and Industry

Each company should appoint a main board director as "champion of learning"; create programs to develop the habit of learning in all employees; provide access to individual mentors or guides; create a skills profile of each employee in relation to his or her current and future life and work; progressively develop external accreditation (assessment for credit) arrangements for in-company courses; and form at least three partnerships with educational institutions and community organizations.

Educational Institutions

Each educational institution should apply the findings of research on the subject of learning to practice; seek continuously to increase productivity and cost-effectiveness; cooperate to develop a statement of key skills and a worldwide curriculum for lifelong learning; identify and match best practice; help create a global lifelong learning network for initial and inservice teacher training; help to develop a new profession of mentors, guides, or learning counselors; form at least three partnerships with business, industry, and community organizations; and value the experience of students as an educational resource.

Universities

Universities in particular should offer leadership to the whole educational service in addressing change; treat the whole community as comprising past, present, or future students; encourage and disseminate research into learning, especially the implications of the new "brain sciences"; encourage the professional organizations to promote lifelong learning among their own members; take account of the requirements of lifelong learning when recruiting and providing induction to new members of the staff; provide programs that allow the accreditation (assessment) of prior learning; and cooperate to harness the new educational technologies in support of the learner.

Governments

Governments should set targets for learning and monitor these;[1] encourage research into, and experiment with, new forms of infrastructure and new funding models to promote lifelong learning; gradually and progressively transfer resources for learning from the providers to the learners; cooperate to develop a global qualification system guaranteed by reliable quality assurance and reflecting the principles of modularization and credit accumulation and transfer; promote the development of the LP; create incentives to encourage lifelong learning (e.g., by adjustments to taxation); ensure that appropriate programs for lifelong learning are available and accessible to all without exclusion and that diverse pathways to learning form a seamless curriculum; encourage the development of cities of learning and develop a system of recognition for these; cooperate to organize a world learning day; and provide special support to families in

disadvantaged circumstances to enable children to start right and to
encourage lifelong learning in the home.

The Media

The media should mount a campaign to raise awareness of lifelong
learning and encourage higher aspirations and expectations; support
the learning process by demonstrating that learning is fun; develop
regional learning channels on radio and television; and provide local
educational support programs (Ball, 1995).

It is important for school leaders to take this information and seek
to implement adult literacy or family literacy programs in their schools
to work toward maximizing the goal of every adult literate.

Note

1. Such targets should be benchmarked against best practice and
include (1) an elementary target for functional literacy and numeracy;
(2) a foundation target for school-leaving proficiency; (3) an
advanced-level target and a degree-level target for higher education
for both young people and mature adults; and (4) a target for learning
organizations, together with target dates for achievement. Learning
targets should be reused in the light of experience and progress.

References

Ananda, S. D., Rabinowitz, S. N., Carlos, L., & Yamashiro, K. (1995).
Skills for tomorrow's workforce. *Policy Brief, 21,* 1-8.

Ball, C. (1995, August). *Action agenda for lifelong learning for the 21st
century.* Paper presented at the First Global Conference for Lifelong Learning, Rome.

Commission on the Skills of the American Workforce. (1990). *America's choice: High skills or low wages!* Rochester, NY: National
Center on Education and the Economy.

Council of Chief State School Officers. (1995). *Consensus framework
of workplace readiness, 1995 revision.* Washington, DC: Author.

Department of Labor. (1991). *Workplace basics: The skills employers
want.* Washington, DC: Government Printing Office.

Ellsworth, N. J., Hedley, C. N., & Baratta, A. N. (1994). *Literacy: A
redefinition.* Hillsdale, NJ: Lawrence Erlbaum.

Fagan, W. T. (1995). Adult literacy surveys: A trans-border comparison. *Journal of Reading, 38*(4), 260-269.

Gowen, S. G. (1992). *The politics of workplace literacy: A case study.* New York: Teachers College Press.

Hirsch, P., & Mortensen, S. (1996). *The effects of an adult literacy education program on workforce productivity.* Philadelphia: University of Pennsylvania.

Hodgkinson, H. (1995). *A demographic study of prisoners: Social factors.* Washington, DC: National Educational Leadership Institute.

Indiana State Library Association. (1997). *Literacy, poverty, and other social problems.* Indianapolis: Author.

Kirsch, I. S., Jungeblut, A., Jenkins, L., & Kolstad, A. (1993). *Adult literacy in America: National Adult Literacy Survey.* Princeton, NJ: Educational Testing Service.

Lchr, F., & Osborn, J. (1994). *Reading, language, and literacy: Instruction for the twenty-first century.* Hillsdale, NJ: Lawrence Erlbaum.

Literacy Assistance Center. (1990). *The New York City Adult Literacy Initiative: Final report 1988-89.* New York: Author.

Lowes Elementary, Graves County Schools. (1997). *Bringing non-English speaking families into the community of the school* [Online]. Available: http/www.kde.state.ky.us/coe/ocpg/dpi/new/grants.html

National Bureau of Economic Research. (1996). *Education and earning potential.* Washington, DC: Author.

National Commission on Excellence in Education. (1983). *A nation at risk: The imperative for educational reform.* Washington, DC: Government Printing Office.

New Jersey Welfare Department. (1996). *Social factors and welfare recipients in New Jersey.* Trenton: Author.

Secretary's Commission on Achieving Necessary Skills. (1991). *What work requires of schools: A SCANS report for America 2000.* Washington, DC: Department of Labor.

Soifer, R., Irwin, M., Crumrine, B., Honzaki, E., Simmons, B., & Young, D. (1990). *The complete theory to practice handbook of adult literacy: Curriculum design and teaching approaches.* New York: Teachers College Press.

Sticht, T. G. (1995). Adult education for family literacy. *Adult Learning, 7*(2), 23-24.

UNISYS. (1996). *The problem of illiteracy in the workplace.* New York: Author.

Wisconsin State Employment Service. (1996). *Education and unemployment/underemployment.* Madison: Author.

CHAPTER **7**

Every School Safe

By the year 2000, every school in the United States
will be free of drugs, violence, and the unauthorized
presence of firearms and alcohol and will offer a dis-
ciplined environment conducive to learning.
(Goals 2000: Educate America Act of 1994)

Growing violence, chaos in classrooms, and access to drugs are a regular part of the school day for an increasing number of students. Consider some of the obstacles facing our schools. Gunshot wounds are one of the leading causes of death among high school students in the United States, second only to motor vehicle deaths. Fifteen percent of all students report the presence of gangs in their schools. At least 30% of students nationwide find it easy to obtain cocaine. Forty-four percent of all teachers report that student misconduct interferes substantially with their teaching (Department of Education, 1996b).

Frequently, the violence in a community spills into the schools. Although the situation in some schools and neighborhoods is more serious than in others, creating a safe, disciplined, and drug-free learning environment is a challenge for all schools. Increasing the graduation rate, improving student achievement in challenging subject matter, and ensuring the ability of our students to compete in a world economy and to carry out their responsibilities of citizenship will be much more difficult to achieve if our schools and neighborhoods are unsafe for our children.

Whether a school is urban, suburban, or rural, several questions can be asked to help understand how it may be affected by violence, drugs, and class disruptions: How many students feel unsafe at school? Are acts of violence frequent? What is the overall drug use in schools? Is the sale of drugs in school a frequent occurrence? Are student disruptions of class perceived to be a problem by teachers and students? What violences are committed that relate to race, class, and gender? Answers to these questions can provide valuable clues to what kinds of problems exist in our schools and what school administrators can do to make our schools violence-free, drug-free, and disciplined environments conducive to learning.

Research: School Violence and Alcohol and Drug Use

There has been a plethora of research and professional literature dealing with violence, drug use, and discipline problems in our schools. A number of studies and reports bear directly on the questions posed earlier. We have chosen several reports and studies for examination here on the basis of their timeliness and their importance to education stakeholders. Some of these reports have been highly visible, whereas others are less well known.

In addition to a desire to reduce overall student drug and alcohol use, reducing the sale of drugs at school is an indicator of progress toward Goal 7.

Although schools cannot be held solely accountable for student behavior that takes place away from school, schools do have a major responsibility for eliminating the sale of drugs at school. School administrators, in cooperation with law enforcement officials, need to exert considerable control in eliminating the sale of drugs at school.

In addition to eliminating drugs, alcohol, and violence in schools, Goal 7 aims to increase the proportion of the nation's schools that offer a disciplined environment conducive to learning. Annual Phi Delta Kappa/Gallup polls for the past three decades have identified lack of discipline as one of the worst problems confronting public schools. Minimizing classroom disruptions is a necessary, though not a sufficient, condition to ensure that an environment conducive to learning exists in our schools and that students are learning. According

(text continues on p. 128)

Box 7.1. What the Research Says About . . .

School Violence

◆ The Phi Delta Kappa/Gallup polls on education over the past decade have cited lack of discipline, violence, and drug abuse as the worst problems confronting public schools. Some authorities point out that public perception of the frequency of violent acts may be exaggerated by intense media attention when incidents of school violence do occur, and that most of the nation's schools are safe (National Education Goals Panel, 1994).

◆ The number of crimes committed at or near the 85,000 U.S. public schools was estimated at more than 3 million annually, with 185,580 people injured. On any given day, more than 100,000 students are estimated to carry guns to school (National Crime Survey, 1996).

◆ Nearly 6,000 violent incidents occurred in New York City schools alone in 1995, an increase of 15% from the previous year (New York City Board of Education, 1996).

◆ Surveys of principals from more than 1,500 school districts conducted by researchers from Xavier University in Cincinnati revealed that violence is not solely a problem of urban schools: 64%, 54%, and 43% of principals in urban, suburban, and rural areas, respectively, reported that violence had increased in their schools during the past 5 years (Xavier University, 1996).

◆ Approximately 30,000 students are physically attacked in America's secondary schools each month. Approximately 5,500 of the nation's 1 million secondary school teachers are physically attacked at school each month (National Schools Safety Center, 1996).

◆ Estimated annual costs of school crime, including vandalism, are between $50 million and $700 million. Estimates of yearly replacement and repair costs due to crime are about $250 million (National Schools Safety Center, 1996).

◆ About one in four students nationally reports having very serious problems in school with hostile or threatening remarks among different groups of students; physical fights among members of different groups of friends; threats or destructive acts other than physical fights; turf battles among different groups of students; and gang violence (Harris & Associates, 1993, 1994, 1995, 1996).

♦ Age appears to be an important factor affecting the level of social tension and violence during the middle and high school years. Beginning in 9th grade, there is a steady decline in the proportion of students who report having serious problems with each of these social problems. In contrast to 8th graders, who see these as very serious problems, less than half of 12th graders express the same level of concern (Department of Education, National Center for Education Statistics, 1996).

♦ Eleven percent of 8th graders admitted that they had brought a weapon to school at least once during the previous month, such as a gun, knife, or club. Percentages increased significantly from the previous year for both 8th and 12th graders, and 3% to 4% of the students at each grade reported that they habitually carried a weapon to school 20 or more days in the previous month (Department of Education, 1996a).

♦ Data from state surveys conducted show that in 20 of 24 participating states and territories, at least 10% of public high school students reported carrying a weapon on school property at least once during the previous month (Department of Health and Human Services, 1996a).

Size of School

♦ Urban students are more likely to report having serious problems with hostile remarks, physical fights, threats or destructive acts, and gang violence then suburban or rural students. African American and Hispanic students are twice as likely than white students to report experiencing very serious problems with turf battles and gang violence (Department of Education, National Center for Education Statistics, 1996).

(continued)

Box 7.1. Continued

◆ One in five students reports that the level of violence has de-creased over the past year, yet an equal proportion reports that it has increased. Two in five believe that there has been no change in the level of violence over the past year. A larger percentage of students in urban schools reports a decrease in violence than students in suburban or rural schools. The pro-portions reporting an increase in violence are consistent (one in five) across geographic areas (Harris & Associates, 1993, 1994, 1995, 1996).

Teachers and the Educational System

◆ When teachers are supportive, encouraging, and caring about pupils' futures, students report less social tension and vio-lence in their schools. Among those who give their teacher As on treating them with respect, smaller percentages report se-rious problems with each of the following, compared with those who give their teachers Ds and Fs: hostile or threaten-ing remarks among different groups of students; physical fights among members of different groups of friends; threats or destructive acts other than physical fights; and turf battles among different groups of students (Harris & Associates, 1993, 1994, 1995, 1996).

◆ Students are more likely to report a decrease rather than an increase in violence when they are satisfied with the quality of education and the lessons they learn from teachers on toler-ance. Students who rate the quality of education high are more likely to report decreases than increases in violence over the past year, whereas conversely, low raters are more likely to report increases than decreases. Students are more likely to report a decrease in violence compared with all students when their teachers do a good job of teaching tolerance (Harris & Associates, 1993, 1994, 1995, 1996).

Alcohol and Drug Use

◆ Between 1993 and 1995, the percentage of 10th graders who reported using alcohol during the previous year declined sig-nificantly, from 72% to 68% (Department of Education, 1996b).

◆ Individual states report that some witnessed a sharp decline in extreme episodes of alcohol consumption among public high school students, that is, the proportion who reported having five or more drinks in a row during the previous month (Department of Health and Human Services, 1996a).

◆ According to student reports, alcohol is by far the most commonly used drug. Alcohol is used by more than half of all 8th graders, 7 out of 10 10th graders, and more than three fourths of all 12th graders (Department of Education, 1996b).

◆ Although the overall student consumption of alcohol has declined, overall student drug use has increased. Between 1993 and 1995, the percentage of 10th graders who reported using any illicit drug during the previous year increased from 25% to 28%, reversing previous trends that indicated that overall student drug use had been declining since 1980. Furthermore, additional data reveal significant 2-year increases in the proportion of 8th and 10th graders who reported using cocaine (Department of Education, 1996b).

◆ Students report that they rarely use alcohol, marijuana, and other illicit drugs at school during school hours. The vast majority of students report never being intoxicated or being under the influence of other drugs while at school. Nevertheless, other data indicate that the percentages of 8th and 10th graders who reported using marijuana or other illicit drugs at school during school hours increased significantly between 1993 and 1995. The proportion of eighth graders who reported drinking alcohol at school during school hours also increased significantly over the same 2-year period (Department of Education, 1996b).

◆ In 1996, nearly 3 out of 10 students, and 4 out of 10 high school students, reported that obtaining alcohol and marijuana at school or on school grounds was easy. Thirteen percent of 8th graders, 20% of 10th graders, and 25% of 12th graders reported that they had been approached at school by someone trying to sell them drugs during the school day (Department of Education, 1996b).

to student reports, we have not made real improvement in reducing classroom misbehavior. One in three high school teachers reports that student misbehavior interferes with their teaching (Department of Education, 1996b).

Applying Research to Practice:
Developing an Action Plan

Interest in predicting school violence stems from a desire to prevent it rather than an attempt to control it after it occurs (Rich, 1992). Ideally, if educators and other school officials could determine the conditions that cause violence and the types of students most likely to engage in it, as well as those teachers whose behavior precipitates violence, timely corrective interventions could be initiated to prevent its occurrence. This approach would be far better than waiting for violence to erupt and then having to deploy resources to quell the incident.

Strategy 1: Predict School Violence

Predicting violence in schools is not impossible. In fact, school administrators in the Milwaukee public schools are using a school-violence tool that has enabled them to reduce attacks against teachers by almost 38% in 2 years. The program, Safe Schools—Better Schools, allows school security officials to identify behavior problems in schools and provide resources immediately to prevent violence from occurring. School security officials in the Milwaukee public schools are taking a proactive stance. They plan in advance and anticipate problems.

In the Milwaukee public schools, where violence against teachers decreased from 1,080 cases in 1992-1993 to 665 cases in 1994-1995, the program has a three-pronged strategy. The strategy includes data collection and analysis, identifying problem students, and identifying problem teachers (National Alliance for Safe Schools, 1996).

Collect Data and Analyze Them

Information on violence and discipline problems reported by teachers is collected using standardized incident-reporting forms and analyzed by computer. School administrators then look at where incidents are occurring, their frequency, and whether specific schools, teachers, or locations within schools are showing a pattern of repeated incidents. For example, if a particular school building is having difficulty during the beginning of school or at dismissal, then additional security officers can be marshaled to patrol the school during those times.

Identify Problem Students

Milwaukee public school administrators believe that little is accomplished by simply punishing students who are referred frequently to principals for acts of violence or disciplinary problems. Additional resources are provided to these disruptive students, such as counseling, referrals to social agencies, or assignments to alternative school programs. The Milwaukee public schools provide a variety of alternative programs for weapon-carrying students, those prone to violence, and students with other behavior or learning problems.

Identify Problem Teachers

Identifying problem teachers may sound a bit negative, but some teachers actually precipitate student violence. Much assaultive behavior on the part of students can be diminished with good psychological preparation of teachers and consistent support of school policies and procedures (Goldstein, Palumbo, Striepling, & Voutsinas, 1995). Milwaukee public school administrators observe that a disproportionate number of discipline referrals are made by a few teachers in a school. Typically, 3% of the faculty are responsible for about 50% of the discipline referrals. In response, school administrators arrange for teachers with classroom-management problems to attend the school district's Professional Development Academy to learn how to handle students. On-site follow-up relative to effective management techniques designed for unique populations is also available through the academy. Moreover, liaisons are established between school and service agencies, such as mental health, child welfare, and the juvenile division of the local law enforcement agency.

Another important part of the program is to develop school teams consisting of teachers, parents, school administrators, and the aforementioned service agencies. These individuals agree to be part of a team. The team approach helps prevent cases from being thrown out

of court for being improperly prepared. Teams of educators and social
services agencies working together can prevent that from happening.
Milwaukee public school administrators claim that the Safe Schools—
Better Schools program will work with schools of any size or type:
urban, suburban, or rural. The program provides a planning system
for administering school security resources.

Strategy 2: Prevent School Violence

Violence in America has increased substantially in the past few
years. In fact, the reported violent crime rate in the nation has increased by more than 35% in the past 10 years. That rate of increase
in such a short period is greater than in any comparable period in
history, or at least since reliable records have been maintained by the
Federal Bureau of Investigation's Uniform Crime Reports. During
that same period, the number of reported arrests of young people 15
years of age and under for violent offenses increased by 100% (Department of Education, 1996a).

It is not surprising that the level of violence in public schools is
increasing as well. Violence in schools cannot be separated from the
larger problem of violence in communities. Studies have shown that
the conditions of schools are strongly influenced by the conditions of
their neighborhoods (Ban & Caminillo, 1977; Brown & Altman, 1981;
Gold & Moles, 1978; Gottfredson & Daiger, 1979; Harries, 1980;
Hellman & Beaton, 1986; Rubenstein et al., 1980). Violence in
schools is endangering the health, welfare, and safety of students and
teachers. Students cannot learn and teachers cannot teach in an atmosphere in which fear and anxiety prevail. Some ways of preventing
school violence include toughening weapons laws, dealing with violent
students, focusing resources on schools, and strengthening the system
(Department of Education, 1996a).

Toughen Weapons Laws

State legislation should be enacted and school board policies
should be developed to address violence in schools. Tough measures
should be sought for dealing with violent behavior, especially possession of weapons, and the initiation of a parent responsibility law for
minors possessing weapons.

Establish Weapon-Free School Zones

School boards might consider making their schools weapon-free zones. Efforts to do so would ideally involve the school, home, community, law enforcement, and health services. Strategies would include apprehension, prevention, intervention, education, counseling, and student and public awareness programs.

Following is a concise statement suggested by the National School Boards Association (1996):

> The board of education determines that possession and or use of a weapon by a student is detrimental to the welfare and safety of the students and school personnel within the district. Possession and or use of any dangerous or deadly weapon in any school building on school grounds, in any school vehicle, or at any school-sponsored activity is prohibited. Such weapons include but are not limited to any pistol, revolver, rifle, shotgun, air gun, or spring gun; slingshot; bludgeon; brass knuckles or artificial knuckles of any kind; knives having a blade of greater than two inches, any knife the blade of which can be opened by a flick of a button or pressure on the handle, or any pocketknife where the blade is carried in a partially opened position. The possession or use of any such weapon will require that the proceeding for the suspension and or expulsion of the student involved will be initiated immediately by the principal. (p. 6)

In addition to a written school board policy, the following state legislation is recommended to provide for weapon-free schools: Make it a felony to bring a firearm on school property knowingly and willfully; make it a felony for any person to knowingly allow a minor to carry a weapon to school; provide that any person convicted of bringing a firearm on school property will lose his or her driver's license.

Limit Access by Minors to Handguns

To provide for limited access by minors to handguns, the following laws are recommended: Make it a misdemeanor for any person to allow a minor to have access to a handgun without the consent and supervision of a parent, guardian, or other responsible adult; make

possession of a handgun by a minor without the consent and supervision of a parent, guardian, or other responsible adult a misdemeanor.

Deal With Violent Students

Students cannot learn when they are in fear of harm from their
classmates. Teachers cannot teach in an atmosphere of fear for their
own safety, as well as that of their students. To provide for a safe and
secure learning atmosphere for children, school districts must be able
to expel violent students; transfer students to alternative schools; require schools to report violent offenders to law enforcement officials;
require court counselors to confer with school officials; expand immediate school actions; and take privileges away from students.

Expel Violent Students

Most state statutes provide that a school board can expel a student, age 14 or older, only if he or she has been convicted of a felony
and the student's continued presence in the school constitutes a clear
threat to the safety and health of other students or staff. State statutes
should be amended so that when the principal and the superintendent
can prove a student is a clear threat to the safety and health of other
students or employees, the school board has the option of expelling
the student even if no felony has been committed. School officials are
encouraged to use long-term suspension and alternative schools or
programs in lieu of expulsions.

Transfer Violent Students
to Alternative Schools

Under compulsory attendance laws, states have a duty to provide
an education for all their children, even those deemed violent by the
juvenile justice system. There have been numerous instances when a
violent student is placed in a regular school setting and the results have
been disruptive and even dangerous. To provide a safe and secure setting for all children and teachers, school districts must be able to transfer to another institution juveniles who have been categorized as violent by the courts or whose presence poses a clear threat to others
within the school. Transferring a juvenile to an alternative school for
long-term supervision is a viable option to expulsion. The state fulfills
its duty to provide an education; the school is made safer by removing
the violent juvenile; the community is not burdened by juveniles who
have been suspended from school roaming the streets; and the juvenile

is provided a safe and structured setting in which to continue the education process. For juveniles awaiting trial for violent acts, this would provide a supervised situation while not enabling the juvenile's continued presence at a school to become disruptive.

Due to the expense of alternative schools, such placement should constitute a last step in a continuum of services for violent students. Placement should be temporary, with the goal being to return the student to the regular school setting at the appropriate time. Although the format of alternative programs varies from small informed programs similar to home-bound instruction in some systems to more formal school settings in larger systems, the focus must be on providing a strong academic course of study with therapeutic emphasis. Other service agencies such as public health, mental health, social services, and juvenile justice must be an integral part of the team providing the alternative education program. School districts should consider using Drug Free School funds, drop-out prevention funds, juvenile justice and delinquency prevention funds, community-based alternative funds, in-school suspension funds, average daily membership positions, basic education program positions, and contributions from other agencies to staff alternative programs.

Report Violent Offenders
to Law Officials

School violence is a community problem, not just a school problem (Hellman & Beaton, 1986). Violence in the schools will be stopped only when the schools join with local law enforcement, parents, juvenile court counselors, and other agencies to work together to solve the problem. For law enforcement to be involved in curtailing school violence, schools must report to law enforcement all felonies and misdemeanors involving personal injury, sexual assault, possession or use of weapons, and possession or sale of drugs occurring on school property. Schools can appropriately handle misdemeanors that do not involve violence, sexual assault, weapons use, firearms, or drugs without calling on law enforcement for help.

Require Court Counselors to Confer
With School Officials

Juvenile court counselors should be required to confer with school officials, the juvenile, and the juvenile's parents or guardian whenever the minor is ordered to attend school as part of his probation after adjudication of a crime of violence. Juvenile court counselors should be given the resources needed to work more closely with the schools. The state's juvenile code should provide that minors placed on probation and required to attend school shall maintain a passing grade.

Expand Immediate School Actions

School districts should take immediate actions to make school safer. These actions should address a comprehensive approach to prevention, intervention, and crisis management. Use of school security officers, peer mediation, crisis intervention teams, and the development of policies and procedures governing student behavior are encouraged (Bodine, Crawford, & Schrumpf, 1995; Goldstein, 1995b; Guerra, Moore, & Slaby, 1995; Porro, 1996; Richardson, 1996; Schrumpf, Crawford, & Bodine, 1996; Vernon, 1995). The following recommendations will expand immediate school actions:

- A student's right to park on school property can be conditioned on agreeing to have his or her vehicle searched at any time by school officials.
- Metal detectors, cameras, lights, hand-held radio communications, and other security measures may be installed.
- Cooperative arrangements with local law enforcement should be arranged to put trained resource officers in schools that need them.
- Parent training and involvement programs should be established or strengthened.
- Peer mediation and conflict resolution programs for students and teachers should be established.
- Rules governing student behavior should be established, communicated, and enforced.
- Warrants against students who commit violent acts in schools should be sought.
- Rewards for information leading to the confiscation of weapons, drugs, firearms, and other dangerous items should be offered.
- Anonymous reporting of weapons or drugs or school property should be encouraged.

- Bookbags taken to lockers should be restricted.
- Intruder drills and other crisis management drills should be held periodically to ensure that students and other school employees are prepared for emergencies.

Take Privileges Away From Students

Principals must have the authority to act immediately in ways that restrict meaningful student privileges. No appeal of these actions should delay the implementation of the action. A prompt and meaningful response to student misconduct is an effective way to produce desired conduct.

The department of education in each state needs to adopt procedures to enable principals to:

1. Suspend school bus transportation privileges for students who commit acts of violence

2. Suspend parking privileges on school grounds of students who commit acts of violence

3. Assign to an alternative school students who commit acts of violence

4. Remove from extracurricular activities (athletic and academic) students who commit acts of violence

5. Restrict attendance at extracurricular activities of students who commit acts of violence

Strategy 3: Focus Resources on Schools

The number of dysfunctional and violence-prone youth in our schools is growing rapidly. These students require special attention (Blechman, 1995; Goldstein & Glick, 1995). Additional resources may be required to meet the needs of these students, including more assistant principals, guidance counselors, school psychologists, social workers, nurses, and teachers. Providing for the needs of violence-prone students also includes funding the basic education program, teaching violence prevention, and developing local task forces. Each one will be discussed in turn.

Fund the Basic Education Program

Smaller class sizes to deal with special needs students will require the allocation of additional teaching positions in the regular school program. Many schools are now assigning school resource officers to schools to prevent school violence. School districts that use plain-clothes police officers report significant reductions in school violence (National Alliance for Safe Schools, 1996). Alternative schools and programs must have additional staff members as well, and intensive therapeutic support to serve violence-prone youth. Basic education program funding must be reviewed as "positive prevention," because our failure to serve the special needs population inevitably leads to incarcerations or welfare that will cost taxpayers much more in the future.

Teach Violence Prevention

State departments of education need to ensure that violence prevention is included in the state's K-12 curriculum. Peer mediation, conflict resolution, multiculturalism, media literacy, and citizenship should be part of that curriculum (Bodine et al., 1995; Cardenas, 1995; Cartledge, 1996; Johnson & Johnson, 1995; Pasternak, 1995; Reissman, 1994; Schrumpf et al., 1996; Shure, 1995). The department of education should encourage teacher training in these areas. In particular, the teaching of citizenship skills needs to be developed more fully in schools. Courses should include personal responsibility, cultural and racial differences, morals and ethics, and problem-solving strategies. Merely teaching about these topics will not be sufficient. Schools must develop these skills in students.

Establish Task Forces

Each school district should establish a school safety task force consisting of students, parents, teachers, school administrators, law enforcement officials, juvenile court personnel, local government representatives, and community leaders. The purpose of the task force will be to evaluate the extent of violence in the schools and the community and to develop an action plan that includes both prevention and intervention strategies. In addition to developing an action plan, the two most important contributions of the task force will be to develop a vision within the community that violence can be diminished and to model the collaboration among stakeholder groups.

Strategy 4: Strengthen the System

As noted previously, juvenile violence has increased substantially during the past few years. In some states, the juvenile justice system is not adequately dealing with the problem. Improving the state's juvenile code and creating a statewide center for the prevention of school violence may help strengthen the system.

Improve the Juvenile Code

Each state should examine its juvenile code and the way its juvenile justice system handles crimes committed by juveniles. The review of issues should include fingerprinting of juveniles for violent crimes; submission of these fingerprints to the state bureau of investigation for inclusion in the Automated Fingerprint Identification System; the age at which a juvenile can be bound over to superior court for trial as an adult; and the access by superior court judges to prior juvenile convictions at sentencing.

Create a State Center for the Prevention of School Violence

The governor of each state should establish a state center for the prevention of school violence. The center would function as the state clearinghouse and contact agency for technical assistance and program development. Specifically, the center would perform the following functions: Serve as the point of contact for data and information about the number of violent incidents occurring in schools across the state; conduct periodic analysis of school violence trends and assess the effect of programs initiated and legislation enacted to deal with the problem of violence; and provide direct service to those requesting to establish violence reduction programs in the schools.

Strategy 5: Create an Orderly Climate for Learning

Diane Aleem and Oliver Moles (1993) suggest ways that schools may be able to reduce student violence by creating an orderly climate conducive to learning. According to these authors, research has indicated three important differences between schools that create an orderly climate for learning and those that fail to do so: goals, rules and procedures, and teacher-student relationships.

Establish and Emphasize Goals

In schools that emphasize academic goals, students are more engaged in school work; that is, they spend more time on task. Teachers in these schools have higher expectations for their students and tend to have more positive interactions with them. These student and teacher characteristics make it more likely that students invest more time and energy in academic goals rather than in a peer culture that might sanction violence and disruptive behavior. Studies (Ban & Caminillo, 1977; Hellman & Beaton, 1986) reveal that school violence is much more likely to occur when students feel that grades are punitive or impossible to obtain and feel that the school curriculum is irrelevant. Also, the level of violence increases with class size and the total number of students taught per week. Moreover, a higher incidence of aggression against teachers occurs if the class consists largely of behavior problem students, low achievers, or minority students. This is one of many reasons for the elimination of tracking (George, 1992; Oakes, 1992).

Specific areas of the school program, related to school violence, that should be evaluated include the curriculum and the instructional setting. With respect to the curriculum, the following questions should be asked: Is the curriculum relevant? Does it meet the needs of students? Regarding the instructional setting, significant questions include: Is the class size and total student body manageable for effective teaching? Are the instructional materials and procedures appropriate? Are grades attainable and fair? Are the students tracked by ability or other factors?

Efforts should be made to improve the achievement of all students in schools. Schools must expand teaching beyond the basic skills to include citizenship, effective decision making, conflict-resolution skills, cooperation, and courtesy (Guerra et al., 1995; Hranitz & Eddowes, 1990; Meek, 1992; Williams, 1991). The art of compromise should be modeled and practiced by teachers and students alike. Students need to learn that these are acceptable ways to deal with their conflicts and to meet their individual needs.

The need to reach children in the early years is important. Programs that provide support for young families should be enhanced. Head Start, Follow Through, day care, and after-school care for children of working or student parents should be funded. School districts must become involved in early childhood education by providing facilities and staff. Teachers need to be trained to work with infants, toddlers, and preschoolers. Parents may require assistance in acquiring parenting skills (Elkind, 1994; Hamner & Turner, 1990).

Establish Rules and Procedures

Students and teachers feel safe in schools that have clear discipline standards that are enforced firmly, fairly, and consistently. This can be accomplished through the development of a comprehensive student handbook that identifies expectations for student behavior and outlines the consequences for students who violate the rules. Student handbooks should outline clearly student rights and responsibilities. Suspension and expulsion procedures should be explained carefully, and the appeals process also should be fully described. Because of the frequency of gang activity in schools, the handbook should include sections on dress codes, search and seizure, graffiti, beepers and pagers, and school design (Goldstein, 1995a; Goldstein & Huff, 1995; Landen, 1992; Trump, 1993).

Establish Dress Codes. School boards should consider policies establishing dress codes for students and teachers. For example, the Oakland (California) Board of Education banned clothing and jewelry denoting identification with a gang; expensive jogging suits often worn by drug dealers; and all hats and clothing designating membership in nonschool organizations. The Detroit (Michigan) public schools have implemented a ban on expensive clothing and jewelry. The Baltimore (Maryland) public schools are experimenting with school uniforms. The Dallas (Texas) Board of Education has adopted a policy that opposes clothing and grooming considered distracting or disruptive, and school principals have been given the discretion to determine what is inappropriate (National School Boards Association, 1996).

School boards may enact reasonable regulations concerning student appearance in school. Appearance regulations have focused on male hairstyles and pupil attire. Student challenges to these regulations have relied on First Amendment constitutional freedoms to determine one's appearance. The U.S. Supreme Court has consistently refused to review the decisions of lower courts on these matters (*Karr v. Schmidt*, 1972). Generally, courts tend to provide less protection to some forms of expression (e.g., pupil hairstyle and attire) than to others (e.g., symbolic expression and student publications). Nonetheless, awareness of constitutional freedoms places limits on school officials to regulate student dress, excluding special situations (e.g., graduation and physical education classes). Pupil attire can always be regulated to protect student health, safety, and school discipline. In short, the extent to which school officials may control student appearance depends more on community mores and on the times than on strict principles of law.

Use Search and Seizure Cautiously. The introduction of drugs, weapons, and other contraband in schools has placed school officials in the position of searching students' persons or lockers, and students claim that such acts are a violation of their Fourth Amendment guarantees. A student's right to the Fourth Amendment's protection from unreasonable search and seizure must be balanced against the need for school officials to maintain discipline and to provide a safe environment conducive to learning. State and federal courts generally have relied on the doctrine of *in loco parentis,* reasoning that school officials stand in the place of a parent and are not subject to the constraints of the Fourth Amendment. In 1985 in *New Jersey v. T.L.O.,* the U.S. Supreme Court held that searches by school officials in schools come within the constraints of the Fourteenth Amendment. The court concluded that the special needs of the school environment justified easing the warrant and probable cause requirement imposed in criminal cases, provided that school searches are based on "reasonable suspicion."

Pay Attention to Graffiti. Attention to symbols is an important way of controlling misbehavior. Graffiti is a form of vandalism (defacing school property) and frequently serves as gang symbols. Immediate removal of graffiti sends a message to students of the school administration's opposition to vandalism and gang symbols. It also prevents conflict over potential gang territory, and it tells students and staff alike that the school administration cares about personnel safety and is taking appropriate steps to protect everyone's safety.

Ban Beepers and Pagers. With the exception of students who have severe medical problems or those who are members of rescue units, beepers and pagers should be prohibited on school grounds. Law enforcement officials maintain that frequently students with beepers and pagers are involved in drug trafficking. Undesirable behavior is less likely to occur when beepers and pagers are banned from schools.

Reconsider School Design. School design and facility use can encourage undesirable behaviors. School policy should restrict student congregation in "blind spots"; recommend random spot checks of problem areas, such as rest rooms, locker rooms, and parking lots; and increase physical security with fences, lights, and metal detectors. The least costly security measure is faculty supervision. When administrators and teachers are visible throughout the buildings and school grounds, disruptive behavior is less likely to occur.

Teacher-Student Relationships

Teachers may be able to reduce student violence and disruptive behavior by creating orderly and nurturing classroom learning environments. Quality teaching can avert violence and disruptive behavior in classrooms and throughout the school. A variety of teaching techniques may be used by teachers as they interact with, facilitate, and direct students within their educational settings (Allen et al., 1969; Hunter, 1984; Hunter & Russell, 1990; Lunenburg, 1982, 1994; Wiles & Bondi, 1996).

Use Reinforcement. Research has indicated that if teachers reinforce students both verbally and nonverbally when they participate both in large- and small-group classroom discussions, irrespective of the correctness of their responses, students will participate more often and more actively in classroom discussions (Hamachek, 1995; Harmin, 1994; Smead, 1995). If teachers wish to get students to participate more often and more actively in class, they should discover what is reinforcing for particular students and then reinforce students when they do participate in class. It would seem that the more techniques a teacher has at his or her disposal for reinforcing students, the better his or her chance for getting good pupil participation.

For example, when a student makes a particularly good response, the teacher might say, "That's exactly it," and nod his head affirmatively as he moves toward the student. In this case, he combines one positive verbal reinforcer with two positive nonverbal reinforcers. Such a combination produces a cumulative effect. Examples of positive nonverbal reinforcement include the following: The teacher nods and smiles; the teacher moves toward the pupil; the teacher keeps her eyes on the pupil; and the teacher writes the pupil's response on the blackboard. Positive verbal reinforcement include the use of words and phrases such as "good," "fine," "excellent," and "correct," or otherwise verbally indicating pleasure at the pupil's response. Teacher actions and responses that act as negative reinforcement tend to decrease pupil participation and should be avoided: The teacher scowls or frowns; the teacher moves away from the pupil; the teacher fails to maintain eye contact with the pupil; the teacher responds with "no," "wrong," and "that's not it"; the teacher manifests expressions of annoyance or impatience.

Recognize Attending Behavior. Related literature on pupil attending behavior indicates that pupil behavior can be classified as either work-oriented or nonwork-orientated behavior and that these pupil behaviors can be distinguished from each other (Schloss & Smith, 1998). Two important variables that are dimensions of total teacher behavior are reported in the literature as instructional technique and the immediate effect of technique on pupil attending behavior. An inverse relationship has been found between pupil attending behavior and pupil disruptive behavior (Bauer & Sapona, 1991; Cangelosi, 1993; Larrivee, 1993).

Suggested criteria for recognizing attending behavior include the following: eye contact with the teacher or the teaching media; active engagement in the task assignment (such as reading, writing, or note taking); a positive response to the teaching task; and participation in the class activity. Suggested criteria for recognizing nonattending behavior include the following: The student appears bored, without eye contact with the teaching task; the student appears not to be taking part in the class activity; the student appears to be taking part in an activity other than the assigned task; and the student appears to be responding negatively to the teacher's direction.

Use Anticipatory Set. Discipline of students is connected with the quality of instruction delivered by the teacher. Following is a discussion of what the literature suggests regarding improving instructional delivery and thereby improving classroom discipline. Observers have noted that teachers usually do not spend much time preparing a class for an activity. They frequently say, "Read this story tonight for homework" or "Watch this demonstration carefully" and expect that there will be a classful of eager eyes and minds anxious to learn as much as possible.

The problem that faces every teacher at least twice each classroom period is that of finding introductory remarks (or procedures) that will produce the maximum payoff in learning. What introduction to an activity can a teacher devise that will produce the maximum payoff in learning? What introduction to an activity can a teacher devise that will produce the maximum in subsequent learning?

The concept of *set induction* comes from research on learning and the theory that has developed from that research (Hamachek, 1995; Kauchak & Eggen, 1993). This research appears to indicate that the activities that precede a learning task have an influence on the outcome of that task, and that some instructional sets are superior to others. If some instructional sets are superior to others, then each teacher is faced with the need to find those types of sets that will be most useful for his or her purposes and to modify these sets to fit the specific classroom situation.

Activities for which set induction is appropriate include the following: at the start of a unit; before a discussion; before question-answer recitation; giving a homework assignment; before hearing a panel discussion; before student reports; when assigning student reports; before a film; before a discussion following a film; and before a homework assignment based on the discussion following a film. Examples of set induction include starting a lesson on tone in poetry by comparing a Joan Baez record with Goldfinger with the Rolling Stones; giving an assignment of creating a character as a set for noticing character in the reading of short stories; using the three hats that Lear wore as facilitating sets to understand the three roles that he had and the three stages of his change; understanding executive, legislative, and judicial branches of government by working through analogies to family, school, and the city; studying history from 1700 to 1900 by giving a set for developing "rules of history"; and beginning a unit in physics with a piece of wood overhanging on a desk. The part on the desk is covered with a piece of paper. The teacher gives a sharp blow to the part of the wood outside the desk, and (because of the air pressure) the paper is undisturbed and the wood snaps.

Use Closure. The skills of set induction and closure are complementary. Unless students achieve closure, that is, perception of the logical organization of the ideas presented in a lesson, the effects of an otherwise good lesson may be negated. By using closure techniques, the teacher can make sure that students understand the material and its relationship to what they have learned already.

Closure is not limited to the completion of a lesson. It is also needed at specific points within the lesson so that pupils may know where they are and where they are going. If the planned lesson is not completed, closure can still be attained by drawing attention to what has been accomplished up to the point where the lesson must end.

Examples of closure include drawing attention to the completion of the lesson or part of the lesson; making connections between previously known material, currently presented material, and future learning; allowing students opportunity to demonstrate what they have learned; and developing unsuspected closure by helping students take what has been presented and develop this material into a new, and unsuspected, synthesis.

Employ Questioning Techniques. The use of questioning techniques is basic to good teaching. Questions generally can be classified into four broad categories: initiating, probing, higher order, and divergent (Eggen & Kauchak, 1996; Hunkins, 1995).

Initiating questions elicit an initial response from the student. Once the student has responded, the teacher probes the student's response. Some of the *probing* questions the teacher asks require students to remember facts or to describe something they see. The teacher also asks *higher-order* questions, which require students to make comparisons, inferences, or evaluations or to relate ideas.

Divergent questions have no right or wrong answers. When first asked divergent questions, many students are uncomfortable because there are no right answers for them to lean on. They are reluctant to explore and hypothesize for fear of giving wrong or foolish answers. As a result, they try to pick up cues from the teacher as to what answer is wanted. If the teacher gives these kinds of cues, however, his or her questions are not truly divergent. If, on the other hand, the teacher is not giving cues, some students are likely to feel uncomfortable and uncertain. This should be viewed as a favorable, not an unfavorable, sign.

Establish Appropriate Frames of Reference. A student's understanding of the material of a lesson can be increased if the lesson is organized and taught from several appropriate points of view. A single frame of reference provides a structure through which the student can gain an understanding of the materials. The use of several frames of reference deepens and broadens the general field of understanding more completely than is possible with only one. Teachers can be trained to become more powerful teachers as they are taught to identify many possible frames of reference that might be used in instruction, to make judicious selection from among them, and then to present them effectively (Burden & Byrd, 1994; Frieberg & Driscoll, 1992; Gunter, Estes, & Schwab, 1995; Joyce et al., 1992).

Be Attentive to Race, Class, and Gender Equity in the Classroom. At first consideration, nonequitable classrooms do not appear as violence against students with which teachers should contend; however, when one considers the societal baggage attached to each equity issue, then violent scenes can be brought to mind. Horgan (1995) suggests that, as far as gender equity is concerned, the best way for achieving it is to improve classroom learning generally. We suggest the same for race and class issues. Administrators should assist teachers in creating better learning environments where equity can be achieved. Following are strategies suggested by Horgan (1995) and Lara-Alecio, Irby, and Ebener (1997):

1. Conduct a gender-bias, race-bias, class-bias audit of the classroom (this should include an assessment of your feelings about your own race, class, and gender; knowing ourselves helps to get a better perspective on how we relate to others).

2. Self-assess and teach students to self-assess.

3. Encourage students to set goals and be risk takers.

4. Provide situations where inclusion is a natural consequence of a multicultural curriculum; that is, where special education students are included and where language minority students are included rather than isolated; a way in which the latter can be achieved is through adult language approach to schooling. (To develop a truly inclusive and multicultural environment, total reform of the school curriculum and instruction is necessary. Understanding goes beyond awareness; understanding of others yields support of others and assists with a more cohesive faculty and student body and, consequently, fosters a safer learning environment.)

5. Teach teachers and students to celebrate mistakes, for from mistakes we learn; but teachers and students should also be encouraged to take pride in their successes.

6. Avoid sending negative messages.

7. Retrain students and teachers to think about to what their successes and failures are attributed.

8. Provide positive, honest feedback.

9. Reduce stereotypical thinking.

10. Redirect selective attention.

11. Remember individual differences.

12. Use cooperative learning groups.

13. Teach items in the curriculum that are not brought out in the texts.

14. Focus on math and science.

The assurance of safe and orderly schools requires the commitment of each individual in the school and larger community. School leaders have at hand the facts regarding physical and emotional school violence, drugs, and alcohol. Armed with this knowledge, they have access to many successful programs and suggestions for restructuring their schools to be safer and more orderly learning environments. The importance that attitudes, understandings, and instructional techniques of teachers play in the scenario to reduce violence in the classroom cannot be overemphasized.

References

Aleem, D., & Moles, O. (1993). *Reaching the goals: Goal 6—Safe, disciplined, and drug-free schools.* Washington, DC: Department of Education, Office of Educational Research and Improvement.

Allen, D. W., et al. (1969). *Teaching skills for elementary and secondary school teachers.* New York: General Learning Corporation.

Ban, J. R., & Caminillo, L. M. (1977). *Violence and vandalism in public education.* Danville, IL: Interstate Printers and Publishers.

Bauer, A. M., & Sapona, R. H. (1991). *Managing classrooms to facilitate learning.* Needham Heights, MA: Allyn & Bacon.

Blechman, E. A. (1995). *Solving child behavior problems at home and at school.* Champaign, IL: Research Press.

Bodine, R. J., Crawford, D. K., & Schrumpf, F. (1995). *Creating the peaceable school: A comprehensive program for teaching conflict resolution.* Champaign, IL: Research Press.

Brown, B., & Altman, I. (1981). Territoriality and residential crime. In P. J. Brantingham & P. L. Brantingham (Eds.), *Environmental criminology.* Beverly Hills, CA: Sage.

Burden, P. R., & Byrd, D. M. (1994). *Methods for effective teaching.* Needham Heights, MA: Allyn & Bacon.

Cangelosi, J. S. (1993). *Classroom management strategies: Gaining and maintaining students' cooperation* (2nd ed.). White Plains, NY: Longman.

Cardenas, J. (1995). *Multicultural education: A generation of advocacy.* Needham Heights, MA: Allyn & Bacon.

Cartledge, G. (1996). *Cultural diversity and social skills instruction: Understanding ethnic and gender differences.* Champaign, IL: Research Press.

Department of Education. (1996a). *Report of the task force on school violence.* Washington, DC: Author.

Department of Education. (1996b). *Safe, disciplined, drug-free schools: A report on goals 2000.* Washington, DC: Author.

Department of Education, National Center for Education Statistics. (1996). *School Safety and Discipline Survey.* Washington, DC: Author.

Department of Health and Human Services. (1996a). *Current tobacco, alcohol, marijuana, and cocaine use among high school students.* Washington, DC: Author.

Department of Health and Human Services. (1996b). *Current violence in U.S. public high schools.* Washington, DC: Author.

Eggen, P., & Kauchak, D. P. (1996). *Strategies for teachers: Teaching content and thinking skills* (2nd ed.). Needham Heights, MA: Allyn & Bacon.

Elkind, D. (1994). *A sympathetic understanding of the child: Birth to sixteen* (3rd ed.). Needham Heights, MA: Allyn & Bacon.

Frieberg, H. J., & Driscoll, A. (1992). *Universal teaching strategies.* Needham Heights, MA: Allyn & Bacon.

George, P. (1992). *How to untrack your school.* Alexandria, VA: Association for Supervision and Curriculum Development.

Gold, M., & Moles, O. C. (1978). Delinquency and violence in schools and the community. In J. A. Inciardi & A. E. Pottieger (Eds.), *Violent crime: Historical and contemporary issues.* Beverly Hills, CA: Sage.

Goldstein, A. P. (1995a). *Delinquent gangs: A psychological perspective.* Champaign, IL: Research Press.

Goldstein, A. P. (1995b). *The prepare curriculum: Teaching prosocial competencies.* Champaign, IL: Research Press.

Goldstein, A. P., & Glick, B. (1995). *Aggression replacement training: A comprehensive intervention for aggressive youth.* Champaign, IL: Research Press.

Goldstein, A. P., & Huff, C. R. (1995). *The gang intervention handbook.* Champaign, IL: Research Press.

Goldstein, A. P., Palumbo, J., Striepling, S., & Voutsinas, A. M. (1995). *Break it up: A teacher's guide to managing student aggression.* Champaign, IL: Research Press.

Gottfredson, G. D., & Daiger, D. C. (1979). *Disruption in six hundred schools: The social ecology of personal victimization in the nation's public schools.* Baltimore, MD: Johns Hopkins University, Center for Social Organization of Schools.

Guerra, N. G., Moore, A., & Slaby R. G. (1995). *Viewpoints: A guide to conflict resolution and decision making for adolescents.* Champaign, IL: Research Press.

Gunter, M. A., Estes, T. H., & Schwab, J. (1995). *Instruction: A models approach* (2nd ed.). Needham Heights, MA: Allyn & Bacon.

Hamachek, D. (1995). *Psychology in teaching, learning, and growth* (5th ed.). Needham Heights, MA: Allyn & Bacon.

Hamner, T. J., & Turner, P. H. (1990). *Parenting in contemporary society* (2nd ed.). Needham Heights, MA: Allyn & Bacon.

Harmin, M. (1994). *Inspiring active learning: A handbook for teachers.* Alexandria, VA: Association for Supervision and Curriculum Development.

Harries, K. D. (1980). *Crime and environment.* Springfield, IL: Charles C. Thomas.

Harris & Associates. (1993). *The Metropolitan Life survey of the American teacher: Violence in America's public schools.* New York: Author.

Harris & Associates. (1994). *The Metropolitan Life survey of the American teacher: Violence in America's public schools—The family perspective.* New York: Author.

Harris & Associates. (1995). *The Metropolitan Life Survey of the American Teacher: 1984-1995: Old problems, new challenges.* New York: Author.

Harris & Associates. (1996). *The Metropolitan Life survey of the American teacher: Violence in America's public schools revisited.* New York: Author.

Hellman, D. A., & Beaton, S. (1986). The pattern of violence in urban public schools: The influence of school and community. *Journal of Research in Crime and Delinquency, 23,* 102-127.

Horgan, D. D. (1995). *Achieving gender equity: Strategies for the classroom.* Boston: Allyn & Bacon.

Hunkins, F. P. (1995). *Teaching thinking through effective questioning.* Norwood, MA: Christopher-Gordon.

Hunter, M. (1984). *Mastery teaching.* El Segundo, CA: TIP.

Hunter, M., & Russell, D. (1990). *Mastery coaching and supervision.* Thousand Oaks, CA: Corwin Press.

Hranitz, J. R., & Eddowes, E. A. (1990). Violence: A crisis in homes and schools. *Childhood Education, 67*(1), 4-7.

Johnson, D. W., & Johnson, R. T. (1995). *Reducing school violence through conflict resolution.* Alexandria, VA: Association for Supervision and Curriculum Development.

Joyce, B. R., et al. (1992). *Models of teaching* (4th ed.). Needham Heights, MA: Allyn & Bacon

Kauchak, D. P., & Eggen, P. D. (1993). *Learning and teaching: Research-based methods* (2nd ed.). Needham Heights, MA: Allyn & Bacon.

Karr v. Schmidt. (1972). 401 U.S. 1201.

Landen, W. (1992). Violence in our schools: What can we do? Updating school board policies. *American School Board Journal, 23*(1), 1-5.

Larrivee, B. (1993). *Strategies for effective classroom management: Creating a collaborative climate—Teacher's handbook.* Needham Heights, MA: Allyn & Bacon.

Lara-Alecio, R., Irby, B. J., & Ebener, R. (1997). Developing academically supportive behaviors among Hispanic parents: What elementary school teachers and supervisors can do. *Preventing School Failure, 42*(1), 27-32.

Lunenburg, F. C. (1982, December). The durable half-dozen in instruction. *Illinois Principal,* pp. 17-19.

Lunenburg, F. C. (1994). *Improving instruction: Teaching skills.* South Orange, NJ: Educational Consultants.

Meek, M. (1992). The peacekeepers: Students use mediation skills to resolve conflict. *Teaching Tolerance, 1,* 46-52.

National Alliance for Safe Schools. (1996). *Safe schools—Better schools.* Eastsound, WA: Author.

National Crime Survey. (1996). *Crimes committed on school grounds.* Washington, DC: Author.

National Education Goals Panel. (1994). *The national education goals report: Building a nation of learners.* Washington, DC: Author.

National School Boards Association. (1996). *National education policy reference manual.* Alexandria, VA: Author.

National School Safety Center. (1996). *School violence overview: National statistics report.* Malibu, CA: Department of Education and Pepperdine University.

New Jersey v. T.L.O. (1985). 469 U.S. 325.

New York City Board of Education. (1996). *Report on school violence in the New York City public schools.* New York: Author.

Oakes, J. (1992). *Keeping track.* New York: McGraw-Hill.

Pasternak, M. G. (1995). *Helping kids learn multicultural concepts: A handbook of strategies.* Champaign, IL: Research Press.

Porro, B. (1996). *Talk it out: Conflict resolution in the elementary classroom.* Alexandria, VA: Association for Supervision and Curriculum Development.

Reissman, R. (1994). *The evolving multicultural curriculum.* Alexandria, VA: Association for Supervision and Curriculum Development.

Rich, J. M. (1992). Predicting and controlling school violence. *Contemporary Education, 64*(1), 35.

Richardson, R. C. (1996). *Connecting with others: Lessons for teaching social and emotional competence.* Champaign, IL: Research Press.

Rubenstein, H., et al. (1980). *The link between crime and the building environment: The current state of knowledge.* Washington, DC: National Institute of Justice.

Schrumpf, F., Crawford, D. K., & Bodine, R. J. (1996). *Peer mediation: Conflict resolution in schools.* Champaign, IL: Research Press.

Schloss, P., & Smith, M. A. (1998). *Applied behavior analysis in the classroom* (2nd ed.). Needham Heights, MA: Allyn & Bacon.

Shure, M. B. (1995). *ICPS I can problem solve: An interpersonal cognitive problem-solving program for children.* Champaign, IL: Research Press.

Smead, R. (1995). *Skills and techniques for group work with children and adolescents.* Champaign, IL: Research Press.

Trump, K. S. (1993). Tell teen gangs: School's out. *American School Board Journal, 180,* 39-42.

Vernon, A. (1995). *Thinking, feeling, behaving: An emotional education curriculum.* Champaign, IL: Research Press.

Wiles, J., & Bondi, J. (1996). *Supervision: A guide to practice.* Englewood Cliffs, NJ: Prentice Hall.

Williams, S. K. (1991). We can work it out: Schools are turning to conflict resolution to help stop the violence. *Teacher Magazine, 3*(2), 22-23.

Xavier University. (1996). *School violence studies.* Cincinnati, OH: Author.

CHAPTER **8**

More Parents Involved

*By the year 2000, every school will promote partner-
ships that will increase parental involvement and
participation in promoting the social, emotional,
and academic growth of children.*
(Goals 2000: Educate America Act of 1994)

The importance of effective home-school partnerships has been identified as a critical factor in the academic success of students. It appears
that parents who have high expectations for their children's achievement (Gottfried & Gottfried, 1989; Marjoribanks, 1988; Parsons,
Adler, & Kaczala, 1982; Seginer, 1983, 1986; Thompson, Alexander,
& Entwisle, 1988), participate in school activities (Epstein, 1985;
Linney & Vernberg, 1983; Stevenson & Baker, 1987), offer encouragement (Grolnick & Slowiaczek, 1994; Holloway & Hess, 1982; Sigel,
1982; Stevenson et al., 1990), and provide positive home learning
environments (Epstein, 1987; Steinberg, Lamborn, Dornbusch, &
Darling, 1992; Stevenson & Baker, 1987) influence the pupils' academic achievement.

Research: Models of
Parent Involvement

Jerold Bauch (1994) developed a category system to classify or
describe ways parents are or should be involved in promoting the

social, emotional, and academic growth of children. The value of a model or category system is in representing the range and type of activities that might be incorporated in parent involvement programs. These categories can be used by school personnel as a framework for developing, evaluating, and redesigning parent involvement programs in schools. Seven parent involvement models are discussed in this section: Gordon's systems approach, the SDC study, Berger's role categories, Chavkin and Williams's parent involvement roles, Honig's early childhood education model, the Jones levels of parent involvement, and Epstein's typologies.

Gordon's Systems Approach

Ira Gordon (1979) developed a useful way of describing parent involvement. His categories are based on the institutions that would be influenced by the involvement. Gordon described four levels of parent involvement in his social systems model. The *microsystem,* the child and family, is strongly influential on the development and school success of the child but requires enormous effort and energy to change. The *mesosystem* encompasses the neighborhood institutions such as schools, recreation, and stores. The nature and quality of these affect the family and the child in less direct ways. The *exosystem* consists of an examination of local policies. For example, family leave policy of employers and the availability of social services from a community agency have an influence on the quality of family life. The *macrosystem,* Gordon's final system, represents the major social, economic, and political aspects of the larger society. In Gordon's view, changes at this level have the potential for affecting large numbers of children and families.

Gordon's (1979) systems model creates a paradox of priorities for parent involvement programs. Should a school plan a series of one-on-one conferences with each parent concerning effective child management strategies or spend a comparable amount of time helping a community agency develop neighborhood support groups for abusive parents? Would it be better to conduct a Saturday workshop on family literacy for a few parents or write a brochure on the importance of literacy that can be disseminated to all parents in the school district?

Another set of Gordon's (1979) categories narrows the focus to roles that parents can or should play when they interact with schools. These role categories are: teach own child, decision maker, classroom

---

Box 8.1. What the Research Says

◆ System Development Corporation (SDC), a California-based research firm, conducted a large-scale study of parent involvement categories (Lyons, Robbins, & Smith, 1983). The researchers found several practices that fell into six categories: home-school relations, home-based instruction, school support, instruction at school, parent education, and advisory groups.

◆ Chavkin and Williams (1993) found strong similarities among all groups (Anglo, African American, and Hispanic) in the top three rankings: audience, home tutor, and program supporter. The categories that were ranked lower in interest by all parents in the survey were the less traditional roles: decision maker, advocate, colearner, and paid school staff. The only differences found among racial groups was in minority parents' greater interest in paid roles. Chavkin and Williams conclude that parents are interested in all seven roles, and that their overall interest in parent involvement in schools is high.

◆ Much of the current interest in parent involvement began in research done with early childhood education programs (Epstein, Schweinhart, & McAdoo, 1997).

---

volunteer, paraprofessional, adult educator, and adult learner. These roles would have multiple effects. The parent would be influenced and so would others who have contact with family members. According to Gordon, this is the ultimate transaction—all gain from the association.

The SDC Study

System Development Corporation (SDC), a California-based research firm, conducted a large-scale study of parent involvement categories (Lyons, Robbins, & Smith, 1983). Fifty-seven projects supported by several federal grants were studied to determine how parents

◆ The Jones levels were used as a framework in a study of half of the school districts in Indiana sponsored by the Lilly Middle Grades Improvement Project (MGIP). Most schools had examples of parent involvement in Level 1. Many MGIP schools had some forms of Level 2 and 3 involvement. No schools had pure Level 4 participation (Jones, 1993).

◆ The researchers were concerned that these early status studies did not provide much insight into what schools might do to encourage more extensive parent involvement (Connors & Epstein, 1994; Dauber & Epstein, 1993; Epstein & Connors, 1994).

◆ Home-based parental involvement is reported to have a positive, significant effect on achievement (Bermudez & Padron, 1988; Chavkin & Williams, 1988; Comer, 1986; Dornbusch & Ritter, 1988).

◆ It is necessary for language minority parents to be involved in their children's education for the reinforcement of native language development and for communication of high expectations and emotional support regarding academic achievement (Crawford, 1989).

were actually involved in schools. The researchers found several practices, which fell into six categories: home-school relations, home-based instruction, school support, instruction at school, parent education, and advisory groups.

The SDC categories, derived from a large sample of programs with parent involvement components, constitute a solid description of the status of parent involvement in the 1970s. Since the Elementary and Secondary Education Act of 1965 and its reauthorization— Improving America's School Act of 1994—most federally funded projects mandate parent involvement. Project guidelines often specify the kinds of parent involvement required. For example, Title I (Chapter 1), Follow Through, and others require parent advisory groups.

There had been few precedents for involving parents in such collaborative roles before these rules were imposed on schools using federal funds. SDC confirmed that parents were being involved effectively in the six categories. Many of the expectations for federal programs continue to use the range of activities described in the SDC study.

Berger's Role Categories

Eugenia Hepworth Berger (1991), in her popular book *Parents as Partners in Education,* presents six roles that parents can or should play in their involvement with their child's school. They include parents as teachers of their own children, parents as spectators, parents as employed resources, parents as temporary volunteers, parents as volunteer resources, and parents as policymakers.

There is considerable overlap in Berger's (1991) roles and those of Gordon (1979). The Berger categories focus on what parents might do at home, at school, and in other institutions. Absent from Berger's categories is a focus on parent education, present in Gordon's list. Berger's roles are descriptive of activities that exist in the traditional school. In her book, Berger describes additional activities and relationships that can build the home-school partnership.

Chavkin and Williams's
Parent Involvement Roles

Nancy Feyl Chavkin and David Williams (1993) surveyed 2,967 parents to determine their interest in various school involvement roles. They asked parents to rank their interest in the following seven roles: paid school staff, audience, decision maker, program supporter, advocate, home tutor, and colearner.

The data were analyzed according to parent ethnicity. Chavkin and Williams (1993) found strong similarities among all groups (Anglo, African American, and Hispanic) in the top three rankings: audience, home tutor, and program supporter. The categories that were ranked lower in interest by all parents in the survey were the less traditional roles: decision maker, advocate, colearner, and paid school staff. The only differences found among racial groups was in minority parents' greater interest in paid roles. Chavkin and Williams conclude that parents are interested in all seven roles, and that their overall interest in parent involvement in schools is high.

Honig's Early Childhood Education Model

Much of the current interest in parent involvement began in research done with early childhood education programs. Alice Honig (1990) classified the kinds of parent involvement efforts reported in the literature. Her seven categories include home visitation (a staff member works with parents in the home); parent group meetings (usually for parent education purposes); home visits for interagency linkages (the home start model); program-articulated home visits (for parents of children enrolled in preschool programs); parents as teachers (sharing duties in cooperative preschools or for parent education purposes); home follow-up on television viewing (based on *Sesame Street* or special-purpose TV programs); and omnibus programs (designed for total education, health, and social service effect on the entire family).

As with many early childhood education programs, the activities described by Honig (1990) include a heavy emphasis on learning opportunities for parents. The general role for parents with very young children is that of learner. Activities were designed to provide information, knowledge, and skill to these parents.

Jones's Levels of Parent Involvement

Bruce Jones (1989) describes parent involvement in schools in four levels. Jones does not consider his levels hierarchical.

Level 1: Traditional

This level includes parent-teacher association meetings and volunteer fund raising.

Level 2: Receives Information

This involves newsletters or other means of communication with parents about students, budget, curriculum and instruction, and other school and classroom activities.

Level 3: Involvement at School

This area involves paid volunteers for a variety of school activities, such as tutoring, hall monitors, cafeteria helper, chaperoning, and advisory group membership.

Level 4: Decision Making

The activities associated with Level 4 include direct participation in hiring faculty and staff, curriculum development, budgeting, and program evaluation.

The Jones (1989) levels were used as a framework in a study of half of the school districts in Indiana sponsored by the Lilly Middle Grades Improvement Project (MGIP). Most schools had examples of parent involvement in Level 1. Many MGIP schools had some forms of Level 2 and 3 involvement. No schools had pure Level 4 participation (Jones, 1993). Although the Jones levels are not hierarchical, Levels 1, 2, and 3 are traditional programs planned by teachers in which parents play a passive role in school activities. In the first three levels, there is no implied partnership between parents and school personnel. Only in level 4 do parents have joint roles to play where their participation can directly influence school programs and practices.

Epstein's Typologies

Joyce Epstein (1985, 1987) and her colleagues at the Center on Families, Communities, Schools, and Children's Learning at Johns Hopkins University provide a departure from the descriptive categories of parent involvement in schools found in other models. The researchers were concerned that these early status studies did not provide much insight into what schools might do to encourage more extensive parent involvement (Connors & Epstein, 1994; Dauber & Epstein, 1993; Epstein & Connors, 1994). Epstein presents six typologies of parent involvement. These typologies are a major construct of the Center on Families, Communities, Schools, and Children's Learning and provide a framework that schools can use to expand parent involvement programs.

Type 1: Parenting

This refers to schools helping to improve parents' understanding of adolescent development, parenting skills, and the conditions at home for learning. The school also seeks to improve its own understanding of the families of its students. Activities and ideas in the trust funds of the six schools include home visits, family support groups, referrals for special services, social services, providing information to parents about teens, and providing parenting skills for teen parents.

Type 2: Communicating

This refers to the basic obligations of schools to improve the communications from school to home and from home to school about school programs and students' progress, including the use of letters, memos, report cards, newsletters, conferences, and other mechanisms. Activities and ideas include easing the transition to high school (orientation letters, tours for middle-grade students, summer and fall orientations for students and parents), holding back-to-school nights, signing pledges or contracts with parents, using phone and mail communications (including newsletters), holding conferences, and providing information on school policies and programs.

Type 3: Volunteering

This refers to the involvement in school of parent and community volunteers and the involvement of parents and others who come to the school to support and watch student performances, sports, and other events. School practices and ideas include volunteer activities (parents help other parents, call about attendance, talk about their careers, mentor students), and increasing family attendance at school events.

Type 4: Learning at Home

This refers to improving family involvement in learning activities at home, including involvement in homework, classwork, and curricular-related interactions and decisions. Activities and ideas include helping parents help students set goals and select courses, providing college information, and conducting career transition programs.

Type 5: Decision Making

This refers to parents and other community residents in advisory, decision-making, or advocacy roles in parent associations, advisory committees, and school improvement or school site councils. It also refers to parent and community activists in independent advocacy groups that work for school improvement. The six school activities and ideas include creating more active parent organizations and increasing the number of parents, students, and community members on advisory and decision-making groups.

Type 6: Collaborating With the Community

This refers to involvement of any of the community organizations or institutions that share some responsibility for children's development and success. School activities and ideas include community involvement in school-linked health care programs, delineating a clear role for families in business-school partnerships, offering workshops at school about community resources, and informing families about students' community service activities and requirements.

The Epstein (1985, 1987) typologies have become the organizing construct around a continuous program of research on parent involvement in schools. The Epstein typologies of the 1990s and the SDC studies of the 1970s and 1980s can be combined to provide an integrated framework for developing, evaluating, and redesigning parent involvement programs in the schools.

Academically Supportive Behaviors Among Hispanic Parents

In a report by Lara-Alecio, Irby, and Ebener (1997), 36 supportive parental behaviors or practices were determined to fall into three broad categories associated with high-achieving children of low-income, educationally disadvantaged, Hispanic parents. The three categories are having high expectations, having a firm belief in the education system, and having a desire to be linked with the school.

High Expectations

The supportive behaviors in this category indicate that parents reported to (1) set high expectations for completion of school, (2) connect education with success, (3) express a desire and act to further their own education, and (4) act as a role model in acquiring an education.

Belief in Education

The parents exhibited 22 behaviors that indicate a belief in and support of the education system. Their homes were images of the school. They emphasized the importance of reading, read with their children, conducted storytelling sessions, played school with their children, provided problems for solving, acted as an encourager, dem-

onstrated a caring attitude, structured time, established limits, provided feedback, reinforced successes through rewards, taught children
to write, monitored television viewing, taught social skills, taught good
manners, assisted with math and projects, provided books and arts
and crafts materials, exposed children to different learning experiences, provided emotional support, allowed children to make choices,
and restricted leisure time activity for misbehavior.

Parents as a Home-School Link

Parents were found to play a major role in the home-school link.
Parents stayed informed about their child's education. They solicited
information about school from their children, participated in school
activities, took a leadership role in school organizations, volunteered
in classrooms, met teachers early in the year, helped in solving problems at school with their children, attended parent-teacher conferences, and interacted with their children about their day at school.

Applying Research to Practice: Developing an Action Plan

The literature is replete with programs that have been effective at
increasing parent involvement in schools. We discuss a few selected
strategies for initiating plans for restructuring in the area of parent
involvement. The strategies span all grade levels from preschool to
high school.

Strategy 1: Consider Developing a Center on Families Partnership

Epstein and colleagues (Connors & Epstein, 1994; Dauber &
Epstein, 1993; Epstein & Connors, 1994; Hollifield, 1995) have implemented a program developed by the Center on Families, Communities, Schools, and Children's Learning (Center on Families) in Baltimore high schools. The researchers provide a list of basic practices
based on the six Epstein (1985, 1987) typologies presented earlier.

Type 1: School Help for Families

Develop a lasting set of workshops on key issues in adolescent development. This could be a videotaped series, developed with the help of a local cable company, community or technical college, or the high school's media department. The guidance office could take leadership for these activities, working with the action team, perhaps using the tapes as a forum for a parent workshop series. The tapes could be made available to families through the school, the library, or for free at local video stores on a checkout basis.

Type 2: School-Home Communication

Include students in parent-teacher conferences. Develop one-page guidelines for parents and teens to prepare for the conference. The guidelines would help parents and teens identify common concerns, interests, and talents to discuss with teachers during the conference. The conference could also focus on students' goals and how the teacher and parent could better assist the student.

Type 3: Family Help for Schools

One member of the action team or a parent and teacher as co-chairs could coordinate parent and community volunteers with school and teacher needs for help. Encourage many to participate by allowing work to be done at home or at school, on the weekends, or before or after regular school hours. Encourage teachers to be creative in their requests for assistance so that the many skills and interests of parents and community members can be tapped.

Type 4: Involvement in
Learning Activities at Home

Design interactive homework that requires students to talk to someone at home about something interesting that they are learning in class or about important school decisions. The homework activity is the student's responsibility, but a parent or other family or community member is used as a *reference source* or *audience* for the student. This enables students to share ideas at the same time that families are informed about the students' curricula and learning activities.

Type 5: Involvement in Governance,
Decision Making, and Advocacy

Invite parents and students to become members of school committees or councils to review curriculum or specific school policies. To encourage diverse representation, ask a more experienced parent or student leader to be a "buddy" to a less experienced parent or student.

Type 6: Collaboration and Exchanges
With the Community

Develop a community resource directory, perhaps in cooperation with the school nurse or with a member of the chamber of commerce or other group, that gives parents and students information on community agencies that can help with health issues, job training, and summer or part-time employment for teens and other areas of need for families and students.

Strategy 2: Consider the Establishment of Parent Centers

The establishment of parent centers in schools has been gaining momentum in the past 10 years (Johnson, 1994). The program has gone largely unnoticed and undocumented amid such school reform movements as restructuring, site-based management, and choice. Parent centers represent a profound change in the way educators view the role of parents in schools and the way parents view their role in the education of their children.

Parent and family centers have great potential for increasing or improving parent involvement in the schools. They are typically specific locations within the school building where parents gather to decide how they will become involved in the school. Many parents take ownership of the centers, a place where there is no interference by school administrators, who instead provide support. Parents invite teachers, other school personnel, and children into the centers to collaborate with them.

It may be useful to examine parent and family center activities using as a framework Epstein's (1985, 1987) six typologies of parent involvement (Connors & Epstein, 1994; Dauber & Epstein, 1993; Epstein & Connors, 1994; Hollifield, 1995):

1. School help for families (responsibility for health, safety, and development)

2. School-home communication (responsibility for communicating with families)

3. Family help for schools (serving as volunteers assisting teachers, administrators, and children)

4. Family involvement in learning activities at home (involvement with homework, classwork, and curricular-related interactions and decisions)

5. Family involvement in governance, decision making, and advocacy (involvement in parent associations, advisory committees, or school site councils)

6. Family collaboration and exchanges with the community (involvement with community organizations that share responsibility for children's development)

Most parent and family center activities fall in Categories 1, 2, 3, and 5 (Johnson, 1994).

Strategy 3: Investigate the Accelerated Schools Movement

By the mid-1990s, the accelerated schools movement involved more than 500 schools in more than 30 states (St. John, 1995). Furthermore, numerous teams in universities, school districts, and state departments of education have been trained to facilitate the accelerated schools change process. The accelerated schools process is a systematic, locally based school-restructuring methodology that has had some success at involving various constituencies of the school community (Finnan, 1996). Accelerated schools explicitly involve parents as partners in the change process (Hopfenberg & Levin, 1993). The accelerated schools process was originally conceived as a way of transforming schools that serve students in at-risk situations (Levin, 1987).

Although the accelerated schools method provides a systematic process for setting visions, assessing the strengths and weaknesses of the schools, and reorganizing to move the school toward the visions (Finnan, 1996; Hopfenberg & Levin, 1993), it does not prescribe the areas the school should address, either in their vision or in their reorganization, although an emphasis is placed on parents' involvement in the training literature (Hopfenberg & Levin, 1993). Each of the schools organized cadres (teams of teachers and possible others in the school community) to focus on improving parent and community involvement in the schools. Thus, each of the schools had, by the end of its first year in the accelerated schools process, an organizational mechanism for systematically working on ways of facilitating parent involvement in the school. These cadres had been working to improve parental involvement.

Strategy 4: Develop Parent Cooperatives

Parent cooperatives, typically characteristic of early childhood education programs, are generally recognized as a significant way to improve the education of all children (Katz, 1994). Parent involvement in schools has always been a central feature of Head Start, Follow Through, Title I (Chapter 1), and other programs.

In the early days of parent cooperatives, parents—usually mothers—worked in co-op programs a few hours a week, assisting a teacher with many of the daily class activities. Teachers offered regular evening parent-education classes to help parents to learn to work with children in the classroom and to support parents in child-rearing roles. Like some parent centers of today, many parent co-ops were owned and funded by a parent organization.

Although parent cooperatives still remain in the United States and other countries, the increasing numbers of employed mothers has resulted in a substantial decrease in the numbers of parent co-ops (Katz, 1994; Shaw, 1992; Taylor, 1967). The national commitment to parent involvement and concern for the welfare of families suggest that it is time once again to create ways to adapt parent co-ops to the needs of today's working parents.

Strategy 5: Consider Focusing on Families, Technology, and the Schools

Around the country, schools participating in Challenge Grants or Title VII Comprehensive Grant programs are focusing resources on minority or non-English-speaking families. Two examples of successful parent involvement programs are provided.

Example 1: Project ExCITE
(Expanded Community Involvement
in Technology and Education)

The principal, school technology coordinator, PTA president, teacher team leaders, EvenStart parents, and family resource coordinator jointly defined three objectives for Project ExCITE:

1. To provide parents the opportunity to understand better Kentucky instruction by participating in hands-on technology supported learning activities with their children

2. To increase parental awareness of available technology

3. To provide training to parents and community adults in basic computer skills

The project has two activity strands: family learning and adult computer training.

ExCITE nights welcome parents to school to participate in learning with their children. In these 2-hour sessions, students teach parents through hands-on learning, demonstrating on-line research, computer animation, multimedia authoring, and hypermedia. On five Saturdays, Cane Run students, parents, and community members are invited to school to "hit the information highway" for a mini-vacation. Using the network, families explore global telecommunications. Teachers are "travel agents" and students are "tour guides." After their "vacation," families create "souvenirs" from their journey using the writing and publishing center. The program targets 50 families.

In addition, the program targets 25 adults from the community and provides eight 3-hour sessions in basic computer skills. Four local businesses joined as partners in this adult training project and sent staff to talk about computer skills needed in the business world: Rohm Haas of Kentucky, United Parcel Service, Zoller Corporation, and Baptist Hospitals. The business partners host visits to their facilities so that the participants may see technology in the workplace (Crab Orchard Elementary, Lincoln County Schools, 1997).

Example 2: Saturday School at Sammons

Saturday School at Sammons (SSS) was located in an urban school district and was funded by a Title VII bilingual grant and fully supported by the elementary school campus administration team. The program ran 10 consecutive weekends for 3 hours every Saturday morning each semester for 2 years under the grant. One half of the parents attended an English as a second language (ESL) class for an hour and a half, then moved to a hands-on computer class for the remaining time. The other half of the parents began with computer classes and then switched to ESL. The elementary students had sem-istructured learning activities during the morning sessions.

Besides the basic English skills of reading, writing, speaking, and listening and learning how better to assist their children, the parents also learned how to write a résumé in Spanish and English and how to fill out a job application in English. The skills were incorporated into the ESL classes and the computer literacy classes (Irby, LeCompte, & Lara-Alecio, 1997). This parent involvement model has been transferred to five other school sites in the Houston, Texas, metropolitan area.

Strategy 6: Create New Options for Parents

We are witnessing an explosion of interest in creating new options for public education and giving parents the power to choose from among them (O'Neil, 1996). Choice programs in the United States include magnet schools, alternative schools, charter schools, interdistrict and intradistrict choice, open enrollment, back-to-basics schools, technology academics, and home schooling. By having choice, parents are likely to become more involved in the school they have chosen for their child than they would be if it had been assigned by school officials.

Three approaches to choice are currently receiving a great deal of attention: magnet schools, charter schools, and interdistrict and intradistrict choice.

Magnet Schools

In recent years, magnet schools have proliferated in urban areas as a result of their role in desegregation efforts (Gamoran, 1996; Steel & Levin, 1994). Moreover, many individual magnet schools and a few magnet programs have existed for some time (Elmore, 1990; Ogawa & Dutton, 1994).

Magnet schools take many forms. On the one hand, they may have a unique programmatic focus, such as science or the performing arts.

On the other hand, they may offer a more limited specialization, such as health care or computers, within an otherwise traditional curriculum (Ogawa & Dutton, 1994; Witte, 1990). Typically, magnet schools draw students from within an entire school district.

Magnet schools can provide a better match between the curriculum and the interests of students and teachers. They often achieve positive school climates, strong leadership, cohesiveness, and sound working relationships. Magnet schools can also create problems in a public school district, however. Selective magnets can become elitist schools, selecting the top students from other schools and weakening academic balances. In addition, costly extra paperwork and teacher inservice may drain resources from other schools (Esposito, 1990).

How successful are urban magnet schools? Do they promote higher achievement? Using data compiled by the National Educational Longitudinal Study (NELS; Ingels, Scott, Lindmark, Frankel, & Myers, 1992), Adam Gamoran (1996) compared student achievement in 48 magnet schools, 213 comprehensive public high schools, 57 Catholic schools, and 39 secular private schools, for a total of about 24,000 students. Achievement was measured in four subjects: mathematics, science, reading, and social studies.

Gamoran (1996) found large differences among the four types of high schools. Students in both types of private schools (Catholic and secular) outperformed students in public schools. The lowest achievement in all four subjects occurred in comprehensive public schools. James Coleman and Thomas Hoffer (1987) report similar results using a national sample of 40,000 students. Magnet schools were not part of the Coleman and Hoffer study, however.

Gamoran (1996) notes that the achievement differences found in his study could be misleading because different types of students attend different types of schools. In particular, Gamoran found that white students and those of higher socioeconomic status were overrepresented in private schools and underrepresented in public magnet schools as compared to public comprehensive schools. Therefore, the question arose as to what extent achievement differences were due to differences among the students and to what extent they were due to differences in types of schools.

When the sample (Gamoran, 1996) was controlled statistically for students' prior achievement, gender, race, ethnicity, and socioeconomic status, most of the achievement differences between public and private schools disappeared. Moreover, in public magnet schools, achievement was higher than in public comprehensive schools in all four subjects. In science, reading, and social studies, these differences were statistically significant. Gamoran concludes that this indicates that most of the original differences resulted from different types of students, not from different types of schools.

Charter Schools

The charter school movement is one of the fastest growing education reforms. In 1991, Minnesota became the first state to pass a law allowing charter schools. California followed suit a year later. By the end of 1996, 25 states and the District of Columbia had charter school laws (American Federation of Teachers, 1996). At the federal level, Congress passed legislation, as part of the Improving America's Schools Act of 1994, authorizing grants to support states' charter school efforts.

Although charter school policies vary, they generally share the following features (Nathan, 1996). In some states, charter schools may be released from district policies and state codes regarding curriculum, instruction, budget, and personnel. In others, schools may apply to waive state and district requirements on a rule-by-rule basis. In return, charter schools must meet agreed-on performance goals and show results—for example, by participating in state-mandated testing programs or mastering statewide curriculum structures.

Charter schools are created through a written, formal agreement between a group of individuals (certified or noncertified teachers, parents, etc.) or organizations (an existing public school, private school, nonprofit or for-profit agencies or firms) and a sponsoring body (e.g., a local school board of education). The requirements for acquiring a charter are dependent on the authorizing state legislation. Charter schools receive public funding, usually based on student enrollment.

The first national evaluation of charter schools since the movement began in 1991 was released by the Department of Education (1997). It is the first part of a 4-year study of charter schools. Researchers report that charter schools tend to be smaller than conventional public schools, serve about the same proportion of minority children, and face serious financial barriers. Furthermore, the study found no evidence that charter schools select more desirable students from the overall student population. In Massachusetts, Michigan, and Minnesota, charter schools enrolled higher percentages of minority students than did the conventional public schools in those states. Moreover, the study found that many charter schools develop their mission around the needs of at-risk or limited-English-proficient (LEP) students. Also, the report found no evidence of discrimination against disabled students, which refutes accusations (McKinney, 1996) that charter schools are excluding disabled students. The report lacks data concerning whether charter schools are performing better than conventional public schools. This phase of the research will be part of the longer 4-year study and will be available in 1999.

Interdistrict and Intradistrict Choice

Magnet schools and charter schools are forms of intradistrict choice (Ogawa & Dutton, 1994; Witte, 1990). This means that parents can select from among schools or schools within schools in a public school district. The most successful intradistrict models now in place are in Montclair, New Jersey, and Cambridge, Massachusetts. These programs have resulted in greater parental involvement in schools and expanded academic leadership by teachers. Community District 4 in New York City has developed an outstanding system of choice using a wide selection of schools, several of which are housed within a single building (Esposito, 1990).

The first interdistrict model was initiated in Minnesota in 1987. Several states have adopted similar policies. Interdistrict programs extend the range of choices by enabling parents to send their children to public schools outside the district in which they reside (Carnegie Foundation for the Advancement of Teaching, 1992). In some states, students have unrestricted choice among public schools. In other states, some restrictions are placed on students' ability to select from among public schools. For example, because of its rapid population growth, Washington has not been able to grant all interdistrict requests. In Minnesota and Alabama, students' interdistrict choices are restricted by desegregation plans in some school districts (Carnegie Foundation for the Advancement of Teaching, 1992; Witte, 1990).

In restructuring schools for the 21st century, plans must be made to include parents. As indicated in this chapter, all parents must be a part of their children's educational program. If parents are unable to understand and support school activities in the target language, then programs to assist LEP parents in doing so must be established by school leaders. Many programs of this nature exist and can be found in evaluations of federally funded programs at the U.S. Department of Education. Other programs of this type may be found on the Internet simply by conducting a search. Information is available to school leaders as they facilitate making parents feel part of the school so that their children's social, emotional, and academic well-being can be enhanced.

References

American Federation of Teachers. (1996). *Charter school laws: Do they measure up?* Washington, DC: Author.

Bauch, J. P. (1994). Categories of parent involvement. *School Community Journal, 4*(1), 53-60.

Berger, E. H. (1991). *Parents as partners in education.* New York: Macmillan.

Bermudez, A. B., & Padron, Y. M. (1988). University-school collaboration that increases minority parent involvement. *Educational Horizons, 66*(2), 83-86.

Carnegie Foundation for the Advancement of Teaching. (1992). *School choice.* Princeton, NJ: Author.

Chavkin, N. F., & Williams, D. (1988). Critical issues in teacher training for parental involvement. *Educational Horizons, 6*(2), 87-89.

Chavkin, N. F., & Williams, D. (1993). Minority parents and elementary school: Attitudes and practices. In *Families and schools in a pluralistic society.* (pp. 72-89). Albany: State University of New York Press.

Coleman, J. S., & Hoffer, T. (1987). *Public and private high schools: The impact of communities.* New York: Basic Books.

Comer, J. P. (1986). Parent participation in the schools. *Phi Delta Kappan, 67,* 442-446.

Connors, L. J., & Epstein, J. L. (1994). *Taking stock: Views of teachers, parents, and students on school, family, and community partnerships in high schools* (Report No. 25). Baltimore, MD: Johns Hopkins University, Center on Families, Communities, Schools and Children's Learning.

Crab Orchard Elementary, Lincoln County Schools, Crab Orchard, Kentucky. (1997). *Community computer fair, community computer classes, and "Welcome to our school meetings"* [On-line]. Available: http://www.kde.state.ky.us/blss/osis/dpr/goals2000/grants.html

Crawford, L. W. (1989). *Language and literacy learning in multi-cultural classrooms.* Boston: Allyn & Bacon.

Dauber, S., & Epstein, J. (1993). Parents' attitudes and practices of involvement in inner-city elementary and middle schools. In *Families and schools in a pluralistic society* (pp. 54-71). Albany: State University of New York Press.

Department of Education. (1997). *A five year study of charter schools.* Washington, DC: Government Printing Office.

Dornbusch, S. M., & Ritter, P. L. (1988). Parents of high school students: A neglected resource. *Educational Horizons, 66*(2), 75-77.

Elmore, R. F. (1990). *Working models of choice in public education.* New Brunswick, NJ: Center for Policy Research in Education.

Epstein, A. S., Schweinhart, L. J., & McAdoo, L. (1997). *Models of early childhood education.* Ypsilanti, MI: High/Scope.

Epstein, J. L. (1985). Home and school connections in schools of the future: Implications of research on parent involvement. *Peabody Journal of Education, 62*(2), 18-41.

Epstein, J. L. (1987). Parent involvement: What research says to administrators. *Education and Urban Society, 19,* 119-136.

Epstein, J. L., & Connors, L. J. (1994). *Trust fund: School, family, and community partnerships in high schools* (Report No. 24). Baltimore, MD: Johns Hopkins University, Center on Families, Communities, Schools and Children's Learning.

Esposito, R. (1990). *Public school choice: National trends and initiatives.* Trenton: New Jersey Department of Education.

Finnan, C. (1996). Making change my friend. In C. Finnan, E. P. St. John, J. McCarthy, & S. P. Slovacek (Eds.), *Accelerated schools in action: Lessons from the field.* Thousand Oaks, CA: Corwin Press.

Gamoran, A. (1996). Student achievement in public magnet, public comprehension, and private city high schools. *Educational Evaluation and Policy Analysis, 18,* 1-18.

Gordon, I. J. (1979). The effects of parent involvement on schooling. In *Partners: Parents and schools* (pp. 4-25). Washington, DC: Association for Supervision and Curriculum Development.

Gottfried, A. E., & Gottfried, A. W. (1989, April). *Home environment and children's academic intrinsic motivation: A longitudinal study.* Paper presented at the biennial meeting of the Society for Research in Child Development, Kansas City.

Grolnick, W. S., & Slowiaczek, M. L. (1994). Parents' involvement in children's schooling: A multidimensional conceptualization and motivational model. *Child Development, 65,* 237-252.

Hollifield, J. H. (1995). High schools gear up to create effective school and family partnerships. *New Schools, New Communities, 11*(2), 26-31.

Holloway, S. D., & Hess, R. D. (1992). Causal explanations for school performance: Contrasts between mothers and children. *Journal of Applied Developmental Psychology, 3,* 319-327.

Honig, A. S. (1990). *Parent involvement in early childhood education.* Washington, DC: National Association of Young Children.

Hopfenberg, W. S., & Levin, H. M. (1993). *The accelerated schools resource guide.* San Francisco, CA: Jossey-Bass.

Ingels, S. J., Scott, L. A., Lindmark, J. T., Frankel, M. R., & Myers, S. L. (1992). *National Educational Longitudinal Study of 1988 first follow-up: Student component data file user's manual.* Washington, DC: National Center for Educational Statistics.

Irby, B. J., LeCompte, K. N., & Lara-Alecio, R. (1997). New approaches to collaborative education. *Thought & Action, 13*(1), 59-68.

Johnson, V. R. (1994). Parent centers send a clear message: Come be a partner in educating your child. *Equity and Choice, 10*(2), 42-44.

Jones, B. A. (1989). *Factors related to effective community based organization intervention in dropout prevention.* Unpublished doctoral dissertation, Columbia University.

Jones, B. A. (1993). An adolescent focused agenda: The collaborative role of school, family, and the community. *School Community Journal, 3*(1), 14.

Katz, L. G. (1994, January). Parent involvement—Co-op style. *Young Children,* 2-3.

Lara-Alecio, R., Irby, B. J., & Ebener, R. (1997). Developing academically supportive behaviors among Hispanic parents: What elementary school teachers and supervisors can do. *Preventing School Failure, 42*(1), 27-32.

Levin, H. M. (1987). *Accelerated schools for at-risk students* (CPRHE Research Report RR-010). New Brunswick, NJ: Rutgers University, Center for Policy Research in Education.

Linney, J. A., & Vernberg, E. (1983). Changing patterns of parental employment and family-school relationship. In C. D. Hayes & S. B. Kamerman (Eds.), *Children of working parents: Experiences and outcomes* (pp. 73-99). Washington, DC: National Academy Press.

Lyons, P., Robbins, A., & Smith, A. (1983). *Involving parents: A handbook for participation in schools.* Ypsilanti, MI: High/Scope.

Marjoribanks, K. (1988). Perceptions of family environments, educational and occupational outcomes: Social-status differences. *Perceptual and Motor Skills, 66,* 3-9.

McKinney, J. R. (1996). Charter schools: A new barrier for children with disabilities. *Educational Leadership, 54*(2), 22-25.

Nathan, J. (1996). *Charter schools: Hope and opportunity in American schools.* San Francisco: Jossey-Bass.

Ogawa, R. T., & Dutton, J. S. (1994). Parental choice in education: Examining the underlying assumptions. *Urban Education, 29*(3), 270-297.

O'Neil, J. (1996). New options, old concerns. *Educational Leadership, 52*(2), 6-8.

Parsons, J. E., Adler, T. F., & Kaczala, C. M. (1982). Socialization of achievement attitudes and beliefs: Parental influences. *Child Development, 53,* 310-321.

Seginer, R. (1983). Parents' educational expectations and children's academic achievements: A literature review. *Merrill-Palmer Quarterly, 29,* 1-29.

Seginer, R. (1986). Mothers' behavior and sons' performance: An initial test of an academic achievement path model. *Merrill-Palmer Quarterly, 32,* 153-166.

Shaw, M. K. (1992). Futuring for cooperative nurseries. *Offspring, 24*(1), 24-28.

Sigel, E. E. (1982). The relationship between parental distancing strategies and the child's cognitive behavior. In L. M. Laosa & I. M. Sigel, (Eds.), *Families as learning environments for children* (pp. 47-86). New York: Plenum.

Steel, L., & Levin, R. (1994). *Educational innovation and multiracial contexts: The growth of magnet schools in American education.* Palo Alto, CA: American Institute for Research.

Steinberg, L., Lamborn, S. D., Dornbusch, S. M., & Darling, N. (1992). Impact of parenting practices on adolescent achievement: Authoritative parenting, school involvement, and encouragement to succeed. *Child Development, 63,* 1266-1281.

St. John, E. P. (1995). Parents and school reform: Unwelcome guests, instruments of school initiatives, or partners in restructuring? *Journal for a Just and Caring Education, 1*(1), 80-97.

Stevenson, D. L., & Baker, D. P. (1987). The family-school relation and the child's school performance. *Child Development, 58,* 1348-1357.

Stevenson, H. W., Lee, S., Chen, C., Lummis, M., Stigler, J. W., Fan, L., & Ge, F. (1990). Mathematics achievement of children in China and the United States. *Child Development, 61,* 1053-1066.

Taylor, K. W. (1967). *Parents and children learn together.* New York: Teachers College Press.

Thompson, M. S., Alexander, K. L., & Entwisle, D. R. (1988). Household composition, parental expectations, and school achievement. *Social Forces, 67,* 424-451.

Witte, J. W. (1990). *Choice in American education.* Madison: University of Wisconsin-Madison, Robert LaFollette Institute of Public Affairs.

Epilogue: Next Steps

Ten years ago, the White House and the nation's governors adopted six national education goals. In 1994, Congress adopted the six goals, added two, and codified the goals by enacting the Goals 2000: Educate America Act. By the end of the century, they agreed, the commitment made by policymakers, communities, educators, students, and parents should be turning those goals into reality. The chapters in this book present a substantial body of information and suggested actions concerning the implementation of the national education goals.

Next Steps

Collaborative efforts to achieve the national education goals usher in a new era of federal, state, and local partnerships. In the past, education policies focused primarily on regulations, categorical programs, and allocating resources for education, rather than on the results that parents, educators, and policymakers want to achieve, namely

- Young children who are healthier and better prepared for school and learning
- Higher rates of high school graduation
- Higher levels of student performance
- Better qualified teachers
- A well-informed, literate citizenry
- Safer schools
- Stronger links between home and school

Setting national education goals has changed the environment for education policymaking to one in which desired results drive policy decisions. The Goals 2000: Educate America Act recognizes that although education reform will remain a state and local responsibility, education reform must also be a national priority. More than ever before, federal, state, and local leadership must work collaboratively to make decisions that will restructure the education system from the bottom up.

The essence of the goals process is informed decision making. Citizens need accurate, reliable information to determine the strengths and weaknesses of their educational programs. The goals process can help communities determine how well they are doing, where they would like to be, and what they will have to do to move their results in the desired direction. This involves the following steps:

- Increasing investments in early childhood programs such as child nutrition, immunization, and Head Start to improve the chance that children will arrive at school ready to learn
- Adopting and adapting the national education goals to reflect high expectations for all learners that covers a lifetime of learning from preschool through adulthood
- Improving the federal student loan programs to ensure continued access to higher education for all students
- Providing support and financial resources through Goals 2000 funds to help states and local communities develop and implement comprehensive long-term education improvement plans targeted to achieve the national education goals
- Making regulatory flexibility a key priority by granting authority to the Secretary of Education to waive certain federal requirements

that impede the implementation of state and local education
reform efforts

■ Assessing current strengths and weaknesses and building a
strong accountability to measure and report progress regularly
toward all the national education goals

Our efforts to reform education in the past have been more fragmented than coherent. For the first time in history, school reform has
a national focus. Now we need a strategy that underscores the critical
roles that teachers, school administrators, and parents must play if our
push for improving the nation's performance is to be not just symbolic
but systemic.

If educational leaders consider the national goals in all campus
and district planning efforts, school reform will occur. If school leaders are focused on goals, then all efforts of the campus or district will
be channeled in that direction. It is up to school administrators to
facilitate full implementation of Goals 2000 and to use the goals as a
reform roadmap for education as the next century begins. The goals
provide leaders with a vision for continued school improvement. They
are an information age blueprint for accomplishing an "age of wisdom" mission. In this book, we have attempted to compile a set of
parameters from which school leaders can work to accomplish that
mission in their schools and communities.

Now that the general education levels in the U.S. are high, educators must take the lead in an information and knowledge "revolution" to succeed in moving beyond the industrial age and mold the
information and knowledge ages into a new "age of reason" called
"the wisdom age." (Achilles, 1997)

Reference

Achilles, C. (1997, August). *President's report.* A report presented at
the annual meeting of the National Council of Professors of Educational Administration, Vail, Colorado.

Resource A:

Summary of the National Education Goals and Strategies for Implementation

Goal 1:
Every Child Ready

By the year 2000, all children in America will start school ready to learn.

Strategy 1: Begin a school and district dialogue by establishing inquiry groups to investigate various effective early childhood curricular models

Strategy 2: Include technological considerations for special needs learners

Strategy 3: Involve the parents to promote readiness to learn

Strategy 4: Provide information to parents on health and prenatal experiences

Goal 2:
Graduation Rates Increased

By the year 2000, the high school graduation rate will increase to at least 90%.

Strategy 1: Alter the instructional environment

Strategy 2: Establish effective school membership

Strategy 3: Develop career academics

Strategy 4:   Develop appropriate and supportive school board
              policies
Strategy 5:   Determine students' learning styles
Strategy 6:   Consider community-based collaborations
Strategy 7:   Establish a case management intervention system
Strategy 8:   Create a mentoring network
Strategy 9:   Establish a school within a school

Goal 3:
Every Student Competent

By the year 2000, all students will leave grades 4, 8, and 12 having demonstrated competency over challenging subject matter, including English, mathematics, science, foreign languages, civics and government, economics, arts, history, and geography; and every school in America will ensure that all students learn to use their minds well so they may be prepared for responsible citizenship, further learning, and productive employment in our nation's modern economy.

Strategy 1:   Teach critical thinking
Strategy 2:   Consider constructivism
Strategy 3:   Investigate current restructuring initiatives

Goal 4:
Every Teacher Prepared

By the year 2000, the nation's teaching force will have access to programs for the continued improvement of professional skills and the opportunity to acquire the knowledge and skills needed to instruct and prepare all American students for the next century.

Strategy 1:   Consider Holmes Group standards
Strategy 2:   Create professional development schools
Strategy 3:   Develop teaching internships
Strategy 4:   Consider Renaissance Group principles
Strategy 5:   Reform educational administration programs
Strategy 6:   Emphasize professional growth and development

Goal 5:
Mathematics and Science Reform

By the year 2000, U.S. students will be first in the world in mathematics and science achievement.

Strategy 1:   Develop curriculum that integrates science and mathematics

Strategy 2:   Develop a plan for science and mathematics assessment

Strategy 3:   Integrate technology with mathematics and science education

Goal 6:
Every Adult Literate

By the year 2000, every adult American will be literate and will possess the knowledge and skills necessary to compete in a global economy and exercise the rights and responsibilities of citizenship.

Strategy 1:   Develop an adult literacy program

Strategy 2:   Establish an agenda for lifelong learning

Goal 7:
Every School Safe

By the year 2000, every school in the United States will be free of drugs, violence, and the unauthorized presence of firearms and alcohol and will offer a disciplined environment conductive to learning.

Strategy 1:   Predict school violence

Strategy 2:   Prevent school violence

Strategy 3:   Focus resources on schools

Strategy 4:   Strengthen the system

Strategy 5:   Create an orderly climate for learning

Goal 8:
More Parents Involved

By the year 2000, every school will promote partnerships that will increase parental involvement and participation in promoting the social, emotional, and academic growth of children.

Strategy 1:   Consider developing a Center on Families partnership

Strategy 2:   Consider the establishment of parent centers

Strategy 3:   Investigate the accelerated schools movement

Strategy 4:   Develop parent cooperatives

Strategy 5:   Consider focusing on families, technology, and the schools

Strategy 6:   Create new options for parents

Index

parent's involvement roles, 154,
  156
SAT test taking, 38
student outcomes, 38
urban dropout rates, 18
urban school make-up of, 18
violence related to, 123
Mitchell, Lucy Sprague, 4
Moles, Oliver, 137
Montessori, Maria, 6
Montessori Method:
  educational philosophy, 6
  origins of, 6
  teacher's role in, 6
Mr. Rogers' Neighborhood, 7
Myers-Briggs Type Indicators, 25

National Adult Literacy Survey, 110
National Alliance for Developing
    School Leaders:
  memberships in, 79
  objectives of, 79
National Assessment of Educational
    Progress, 38, 110
National Association for the Educa-
    tion of Young Children, 1
National Association of Elementary
    School Principals, 75
National Center for Restructuring
    Education, School, and Teach-
    ing, 70
National Coalition for the Prevention
    of Adolescent Pregnancy, 11
National Commission on Excellence
    in Education, 63
National Commission on Excellence
    in Educational Adminis-
    tration, 74
National Committee on Science
    Education Standards and
    Assessment, 42, 93, 103
National Council for the Accredita-
    tion of Teacher Education, 70
National Council of Professors of
    Educational Administration, 75
National Council of Social Studies, 42

National Council of Teachers of
    English, 42
National Council of Teachers of
    Mathematics:
  constructivism and, 41
  goals of, 93
  math goals of, 93, 94
  school assessment plans, 103
  science and math connection, 100
National Education Association
    Teacher Education Initiative, 70
National education goals:
  evaluation steps for, 177-178
  implementation of, 177
  national priority of, 177
  regulation vs results, 176-177
  school reform and, 178
  See also Goals 2000
National Network for Educational
    Renewal, 70
National Organization for Pregnancy,
    Prevention, and Parenting, 11
National Policy Board (NPB):
  administrator reforms, 75-76
  educational administration, 75
  principal preparation for, 76
  superintendent standards for, 77
National Science Teachers Associa-
    tion, 98
Negative-sanction policies:
  driver's license revoking of, 31
  examples of, 30-31
  parent accountability, 31
  technology resources for, 31
New York City Adult Literacy Initia-
    tive:
  achievement of, 115-116
  cost of, 116-117
  employment and, 115
  language emphasis in, 114
  model program, 114
  provider agencies for, 114
  social service cooperation, 115
  strength of, 114
New York City Attendance Improve-
    ment Dropout Prevention:
  budget for, 26

CORWIN
PRESS

The Corwin Press logo—a raven striding across an open book—
represents the happy union of courage and learning. We are a
professional-level publisher of books and journals for K–12 educators,
and we are committed to creating and providing resources that embody these qualities. Corwin's motto is "Success for All Learners."